MANAGING PEOPLE IN ORGANIZATIONS

Applying modern management theory to the financial services

David James

The Chartered
Institute of Marketing

Apart from any fair dealing for the purpose of research or private study, or criticism or review, as permitted under the Copyright, Designs and Patents Act 1988, this publication may only be reproduced, stored or transmitted, in any form or by any means, with the prior permission in writing of the publisher, or in the case of reprographic reproduction in accordance with the terms and licences issued by the Copyright Licensing Agency. Enquiries concerning reproduction outside those terms should be addressed to the publisher's agents at the undermentioned address:

CIB Publishing
c/o The Chartered Institute of Bankers
Emmanuel House
4-9 Burgate Lane
Canterbury
Kent
CT1 2XJ
United Kingdom

Telephone: 01227 762600

CIB Publishing publications are published by The Chartered Institute of Bankers, a non-profit making registered educational charity.

The Chartered Institute of Bankers believes that the sources of information upon which the book is based are reliable and has made every effort to ensure the complete accuracy of the text. However, neither CIB, the author nor any contributor can accept any legal responsibility whatsoever for consequences that may arise from errors or omissions or any opinion or advice given.

Typeset by Kevin O'Connor

Printed by Redwood Books Limited, Trowbridge, Wiltshire

© Chartered Institute of Bankers 1999

ISBN 0-85297-512-0

Managing People in Organizations

This textbook has been written for both students and practitioners of the subject. It has been written to a syllabus drawn up by subject experts, including current senior practitioners, which forms part of the Diploma in Financial Services Management (DFSM) and the Certificate in Marketing of Financial Services (CMFS). The DFSM qualification is administered by the Institute of Financial Services, a wholly owned subsidiary of The Chartered Institute of Bankers (CIB) and is awarded jointly by The CIB and the University of Manchester Institute of Science and Technology (UMIST). The role of UMIST in this partnership is to benchmark all aspects of the delivery of the DFSM, including this text, to first year undergraduate standard.

The CMFS is the result of a partnership between the CIB and the Chartered Institute of Marketing offering a qualification that meets the specific needs of those involved in the selling and marketing of financial products.

Though written to a syllabus specific to the DFSM it is intended that this text will serve a useful purpose for anybody studying for a business or finance-related qualification. Furthermore, this book will serve as an excellent reference tool for practitioners already working in this or related fields. All books in the DFSM series reflect the very latest regulations, legislation and reporting requirements.

Students of the DFSM will also receive a separate Study Guide to be used in conjunction with this text. This Study Guide refers the reader to further reading on the topic and helps to enhance learning through exercises based upon the contents of this book.

INTRODUCTION

In the pages that follow I have tried to cover many of the key aspects of managing people. As you will realize, this whole area is extremely broad and we would need volumes rather than pages to even begin to get a detailed understanding of many of the more complex areas. Nevertheless, when looking at the various sections, you will find some of the more important issues that need to be considered and in each section you will gain a flavour of different aspects of management.

There is a general and genuine emphasis on the practical application of theory to the workplace. When reading about different aspects of management it is, in my view, much more than having a chance to look at various models and theories. All of this is important in its own way but it must be seen in context. This context is about understanding, applying, adapting and making these theories come to life when dealing with real people. All of us are faced with the reality of managing various aspects of a business unit and are therefore charged with 'making it happen' and with delivering (exceptional) results through our people.

In completing the sections that follow it is entirely appropriate that I thank my family for the support that they have given me throughout. My wife, Elsa and son, Oliver know how important they are to me and both have always provided me with infinite inspiration. Since my days of sitting 'O' levels (as they were in those days) my own personal thirst to continue to learn and help others to learn has remained undiminished and, over a time span now in excess of 20 years, my mum and dad have also been with me and supported me throughout. Thank you.

CONTENTS

1

THE ORGANIZATION

Organization is a term that has been defined in many different ways over the years and in some ways the dictionary definition that is acceptable for our purposes is that it is "a body of people organized for some end or work".

It was at the beginning of the 20th Century that many views on how organizations were formed or evolved began to appear. These main views that began to evolve were as follows:

● *The classical school*

These studies evolved around various aspects of formal organization where it was assumed the efforts of people in an organization could be arranged to achieve greater effort and output than if they were left in an unorganized state. This view focused almost solely on the formal anatomy of an organization, and the managerial functions of span of control, chain of command, delegation of authority and responsibility, and functional management. This approach involved every single person in an organization.

● *The human relations school (or neo-classical school)*

This approach developed the early views of the classical school and its formal approach by adding to it the importance of the informal actions of groups and individuals and considered their impact on how an organization can function with these new dimensions incorporated.

● *The modern school*

This approach looks at organization and systems. This means that each organization is part of a larger system and is itself a system having its own sub-system. It therefore follows that each system is viewed as a sub-system and each system cannot be treated as being completely independent of other systems. Logically, it follows, if this approach is adopted, that one organization cannot be treated as being independent of other organizations.

In a later section we shall be considering these views in greater detail.

1.1 Organizational theory

Why are organizations important?

The most obvious answer here is that organizations are important because a considerable part of each working person's life is involved with them. Children right through until maturity spend a large part of their lives in schools or other academic organizations, and are involved in other activities like, for example, clubs or associations. Those who are employed at some stage during their lives spend a large proportion of their week working in work organizations. Then, the vast majority become involved in other organizations involving sport, leisure, recreation or education. It therefore seems that each individual's life is inevitably interrelated with the activities of an organization, and furthermore that organization could not exist without individuals.

The organizational environment

Here we need to be very careful with our definition, and in terms of organizational theory we shall take this definition to be the sum total of the elements that are in existence outside (and outside of the control span) of an organization. Typically these (external) forces can be grouped under several headings, as follows:

- Legal
- Political
- Economic
- Social
- Technological
- Competition

Each of the above headings can be further broken down into local forces, national forces or even international forces. Logically, the local forces could be expected to have the most impact on an organization, national forces having the next largest impact, and so on.

The crucial point to grasp here is that, whichever way we consider the environment in which an organization works, an organization does not, and cannot, operate in a vacuum. Each organization carries out essential activities that involve factors outside of the organization itself. For example, organizations need to purchase goods and services from elsewhere, an organization has something to provide to the community itself, organizations compete against each other, organizations must establish relationships with their workforce, other organizations – this list is endless, and we can quickly see how the action that any organization takes will impact on the environment around it, and that the way in which the external environment changes will impact on the organization itself.

Broadly speaking the ethics that the environment surrounding an organization has on the organization itself depends upon three broad areas:

- Whether these changes to the surrounding environment are helpful or unhelpful to the current activities of the organization. These circumstances determine whether the changes have a good or otherwise effect on the organization.

- Whether the organization itself is in fact aware of the changes in the surrounding environment.

- Whether, once the organization has become aware of the surrounding changes to the environment, it does (if it is given the choice) take any action to respond to these changes.

Usually, the changes to an organization's surrounding environment are complex, as are the changes in an organization itself. It is also quite possible that the change in the one aspect of the external environment may impact other external environmental forces. For example, a change in political approach may well affect the surrounding economical circumstances.

Organization and individuals

For many people, life inside organizations has comparisons to life outside an organization. There can be some similar challenges and pleasures inside and outside of an organization in building relationships with others, for example. However, we can argue that the organizational environment, particularly the structure, can impose some additional pressures on individuals over and above these. Organizations can be a source of stimulation to individuals in their own right, although the stimulating effects can be difficult to measure.

Some managers, even today, hold the belief that an organization is merely a place to work and not a place to live. These type of managers still have the belief that the organization need not provide an outlet for an individual to *live*, and that this need should occur outside of the workplace. Clearly, the vast majority of managers see this artificial separation of work from *play* as being naive and unrealistic.

Within an organization itself there is some inevitable competition between individuals. One dimension of this is the competition for advancement within an organization – some organizations actively cultivate this type of working environment, which can be a positive dimension if an organization is growing, but perhaps more difficult to manage when it is not. There obviously needs to be a delicate balance between individual competition to grow within an organization and this competition not becoming a *battle*, which could become counterproductive both to the individuals themselves and to the wider organization.

All individuals within an organization have their own responsibilities, although members of the workforce at the *lower levels* of an organization almost inevitably have a good dependency on those higher up the organization. In reality, individual's responsibilities inevitably overlap and are not ultimately clear cut. As an organization gets bigger, levels of responsibility tend to correspond with the levels of authority that go with it. For example, managers at the top of an organization are involving some of their team with the decision making process, while concurrently maintaining control over the final outcome of the process and of the relationship with their team members themselves. It can be argued that with the delegation of authority and responsibility, carefully defined areas of responsibility to individuals in *individually sized pieces*, control from the higher levels of the organization can be maximized. If various individuals are responsible for a particular part of an activity, any problems can be quickly identified and corrective action thereby taken by individuals themselves. Again, the reality is that any one individual will not be making all the necessary decisions alone, and the actions that any individual does take in the workplace will undoubtedly affect others. Similarly, any individual will be affected by the actions of other individuals.

Within organizations, there will be groups of people, all varying in size. All of these groups will be different in some respects, and the size of groups within an organization is very important, particularly in terms of the way in which they can be managed. In some ways the bigger the group the more the individual within that group is distanced from the *top* of the organization. Perhaps as a result of this, the individual's anonymity will increase also.

Human communication in organizations

There are three aspects that we shall consider here, all of which shall be explored in greater depth at a later stage.

Interpersonal communication

All individuals have different attitudes, different reactions and different standpoints in respect of any given situation. Each individual perceives any given scenario in a slightly different way – this means that one line of argument may succeed with one individual and exactly the same line of argument could well fail with another individual. For example, one individual may perceive a particular communication as an order whereas another may perceive exactly the same communication as helpful advice.

The language used in interpersonal communication is very important because words and phrases mean different things to different individuals who all come from different backgrounds. There may be resultant poor expression, ambiguity or imprecision.

It therefore seems clear that imprecision in the language used will lead to potentially wider variations in interpretation which can be further exaggerated, with each individually having his or her own psychological and social differences and difference in perspective as well.

The use of language is a very complex area and it can be used in an attempt to convey some precise information or detail. Language can also be used in a rhetorical sense, perhaps to motivate or to stimulate emotion or perhaps to impress others.

For any communication to be effective at an interpersonal level there are some key criteria:

- Any communication given must be based on as much information as possible about the receiver and the specific situation itself. This means that the best approach to the communication, and the *language* that is ultimately used, can be selected.

- Feedback on any given communication must be requested, collated and acted upon so that the ongoing effectiveness of any communication can be evaluated and improved.

- In any organization individuals must be as precise and as consistent as possible in their use of language.

- Individuals, both the communicators and the receivers, must ensure that they give or personally seek complete clarity when imprecise language is being used either by themselves or others. This implies that listening and understanding skills are at least as important as the communication skills themselves.

We should not, of course, merely think of communication as being in words. Other types of communication include the behavioural aspect, which is in itself a very powerful medium of communication and is often relied upon.

Organization communication

The challenges of communication increase as an organization becomes more complex and for an organization to function to maximum effectiveness, all communication activities must be planned, coordinated and controlled to enable information to flow smoothly and accurately in all directions.

As an organization becomes bigger and more complex there are other areas to consider:

- The potential for distortion in communication increases with more individuals with their own personal differences in interpretation inevitably accumulating.

- Some individuals retain (and not share) information as a defensive measure.

- The impact and affect of the various levels of authority across an organization begin to influence how the communication flows work in practice. For example, we tell our line manager only what we want him to know!

- Individuals within an organization may rigorously pursue success in their own duties or responsibilities while not being aware of their responsibilities in terms of passing on information to others.

- The larger an organization becomes the more diverse the interests and interpretations of the groups and individuals within it become. It is here that the necessity of a *common language* becomes much more important.

There are many options by which organizations can communicate: traditionally using channels of authority through managers or team leaders; by involving employee's representatives or committees or holding conferences; perhaps by using more direct methods such as notices, individual letters or news-sheets. All of these approaches have their benefits, depending on when they are used – each approach should not and in reality cannot be seen as an alternative, because they can and should be used as being complimentary to each other.

In any organization, but probably more so in larger organizations, information must be able to flow freely in all directions. From any point within an organization information may be provided in the form of instructions or motivation, for example. Similarly it must also flow inwards back to the provider so that feedback is provided on an ongoing basis. By the very nature of organizations having a free flow of information, this means that feedback is not merely provided *up the line* – it could well be provided in any direction.

Communication as a motivator

It is common sense to most of us that individuals work better when they know what they are doing and why, and have some understanding of how what they do fits in to the bigger picture. It is unrealistic to expect individuals to do something without any sort of understanding or explanation.

Ways in which communication can be enhanced in this way include:

- At a fundamental level, for individuals to be clear about how much time will be involved and how much they will be paid for fulfilling any particular activity.

- Motivational effects can occur if individuals are aware of how they are getting on against any set objective or target.

- Individuals should be kept fully informed and involved in any changes that will be taking place.

- Although in reality not all employees will want to show an active and regular interest or become involved in the organization's policies and affairs, this type of information should be made available for those who do show interest.

- Any attempts at motivating through communication must be well thought out and above all seen to be sincere. Examples here would include organizational publications and consultative activities which arguably have no value in themselves, but become valuable when they express genuinely cooperative attitudes (including those of management, team leaders and team members themselves).

1.2   Approaches to organization

When running a business becomes beyond the capability of one single person to perform and deliver, it has to involve other people. The immediate issue then is to consider how people can work together to deliver results for the business. Organization, then, is one way of considering how work can be allocated among people, whose efforts will essentially have to be co-ordinated. There then becomes some inevitability that when organizing the work and activities among people there will be a need to consider what objectives the business as a whole must have (and therefore what each of its sections or units must have) and which are necessary to meet in order to achieve the overall objectives.

There are many reasons why organizations may not work as effectively as they might and these include:

- Various departments and sections may be unable to contribute in such a way as to justify their own costs and overheads.

- Each part of the business or organization may not be coordinated in a realistic or effective way.

- Inter-departmental activities may not be coordinated, leading to missed opportunities in terms of economies of skill.

- The decision making process may be poor and slow because of inadequacies at managerial level, poor information flows, or perhaps the decisions are actually being made (or not) at the wrong place or level.

There are three main approaches to organization that we need to look at as follows:

The classical approach

This approach was the first to develop and refers to the principals developed by F.W. Taylor, F.B. Gilbreth, Henri Fayol, J.D. Mooney and O. Urwick. These writers thought of organization as a formal structure of responsibilities and positions. The approach rested on an acceptance of a series of universal principals and coordination, lines of authority and responsibility, the functional differentiation of posts, spans of control and lines of communication, all of which should be geared to a hierarchy of management.

According to this view, these principals could be applied to any enterprise, and an ideal structure of organization could be planned, even though practical considerations meant that something less, in reality, may have to be accepted. This approach is, therefore, about a basic need to study and define the various activities involved, to group them into jobs, sections and departments and then to maintain the right degree of specialization, coordination and control.

This approach focuses on the following:

- An organization has broad objectives which are then broken down on a more local level to give a more detailed specification of the work to be done in each business unit.

- Activities of the organization are grouped into sections, the sectional activities are grouped into departmental activities, and so on, until individual activities are determined.

- Authority is delegated.

- Responsibility and accountability is defined at an individual level.

- Employees work with each other on a formal basis, so that each person learns his or her own position within the team and the business overall.

Later on in this section, we will consider in more detail the work of Fayol and Taylor.

The human relations approach

This approach begins with an assumption that alongside the formal organization of a business there will exist an informal one. This means that an organization will and must be regarded as a complex association of various primary working groups or teams, each of which will have its own set of attitudes, codes of behaviour, individual roles and patterns of activity. In reality, therefore, the human relations approach believes that there is a coexistence of formal and informal structures within an organization. The implication here is that what actually happens in an organization can therefore be radically different from what the management of the business or organization believes to be the case. It seems, according to this view, that if you put human beings together, complex interpersonal relationships are bound to form and affect job performance in some way.

Furthermore, although this approach begins to study a person's motives and behaviours for working, an approach to start to consider is running an organization that stimulates a workforce, individually and collectively to cooperate in achieving the overall aims of the business. This view argues that there can be no effective coordination of activities unless people are willing to cooperate and such cooperation is not achieved automatically, although it can be facilitated by the organization itself.

Among the pioneers of this approach were Elton Mayo, particularly in his Hawthorne research (which we shall consider in more detail later on), M.P. Follett and Kurt Lewin.

The systems approach

This approach defines a system as an entity that can consist of interrelated, interacting or interdependent parts and argues that a business enterprise or organization is largely a system of inputs and outputs.

This systems approach involves an analytical study of an organization and attempts to predict the manner in which a system will operate and then try to reconstruct an organization in a different way to try to make it more successful. This approach therefore focuses on the decisions that need to be made to achieve the business objectives and sees the organization itself as a vehicle designed to facilitate decision making.

The decision making process is a key focus for the systems approach because it is felt that through the process of decision making that the organizational policies will be agreed, leading to resultant actions that will determine the future success (or otherwise) of the company. Furthermore, since these decisions require information and this information needs to be communicated, the systems approach not only studies the decision process itself, but also considers the dimensions of information and communication and how these interact before, during and after the decision making process. The communication of information is seen as essential, particularly in a large organization, as without it, it is argued there can be neither cooperation nor coordination of the overall business activities.

An example of some published work on the systems approach is that by Burns and Stalker in *The Management of Innovation*, which looks at the nature of mechanistic and organic systems and the differences between them.

F.W. Taylor

Taylor was a *classical writer* who was born in 1856 in the United States and spent his working life as a machinist or as a labourer.

Taylor's work evolved from his experience in the workplace and from what he saw and observed regarding the inefficiencies arising from relationships between management and the workforce and the tactics of the workforce itself. Taylor felt that, at that time, management did not know what constituted a *fair day's work*, and were not prepared to provide better and more efficient equipment to the workforce to increase activity.

Taylor felt that he needed to try to establish what constituted a *fair day's work* by investigation and analysis which ultimately evolved from a scientific study of shovelling activities and output on lathes. From the first piece of research, Taylor discovered that labourers shovelled a wide variety of materials, and that fatigue in some cases became inevitable. It therefore seemed sensible to determine a correct size of load for different types of materials, and to conclude that different sizes of shovels could be used for shovelling different types of material. Furthermore a *best* shovelling technique was introduced and training provided to the workforce to help them to learn this. In addition, the workforce became incentivized to adopt these new techniques and in the first year of applying this approach, the workforce received a salary rise of 63%, and the cost to the business fell by 54%. The second piece of Taylor's research looked at output on lathes and soon established the need for different approaches in using the lathe when working with different materials. When these various approaches were agreed and established, the workers were able to use the lathes on a much more efficient basis, but they were frequently kept waiting for other tools, materials or further guidance which then itself raised a new set of issues for management (managing workflows, stock control and communication, for example).

Taylor also did some work on the role of the foreman (or team leader), which evolved quite logically from his earlier work on shovelling and lathes. As a result of the more efficient use of the shovels and lathes, the workers found they were waiting for tools, materials and instructions brought on by these technical improvements. This led to management problems of planning and control which seemed to be separate from (but not mutually exclusive of) the performance of the task itself. In Taylor's view the responsibilities for planning and performance must be divided.

Henry Fayol

Fayol was another classical writer who was born in France in 1841. He spent his life as a mining engineer and became in 1866 a manager of a group of collieries at the age of 25. Later on Fayol was to become a general manager. It was in this senior executive position that Fayol realized the need for adequate management ability in his subordinates to ensure that his policies were correctly interpreted and implemented. From these conclusions, Fayol developed an interest in management training and attempted to analyse management and to evolve a series of principles that could be taught and trained.

It was from these studies that Fayol believed that industrial activities could be grouped into the following functions:

Technical

Commercial

Financial

Security

Accounting

Management

Fayol went on to define the following 13 principles of management:

- Division of work, combining specialization with efficiency.

- The need for authority and responsibility to be clearly defined and properly delegated.

- Discipline, where the leaders would lead by example and act in a very self-disciplined way.

- Unity of command, where there is only one boss or manager in any particular area of responsibility.

- Unity of direction, where business objectives should be clearly defined and understood by everybody who then can work together to achieve these common objectives.

- Common interests, whereby each individual employee's interests should be linked to the overall company objectives. In this context, the organization's goals are seen as primary objectives whereas an individual's interests are seen as collateral objectives.

- Remuneration, whereby employees should be *adequately* paid in order to achieve stability in the workforce. In addition, extra responsibility should be incentivized by a higher level of remuneration.

- Scalar chain, which means Fayol proposed a series of line relationships throughout an organization.

- Order, which in an organizational context meant that there should be adequate levels of staffing with various positions clearly identified and occupied by members of staff who had been properly selected for each role.

- Equality within an organization, meaning fair treatment for each employee.

- Stability of tenure, which meant that each employee's job should be secure in the context of the principles identified above.

- Initiative, whereby Fayol saw the importance to encourage individual employees to use his or her initiative.

- Esprit de corps, which meant that Fayol saw the importance of having a good team spirit within the organization.

Another dimension of Fayols's work looked at the various qualities required from a manager and he saw *management* as consisting of:

Planning, organization, commanding, controlling and coordinating.

Fayol, then, saw management as a specialist task in itself, which he felt required very close scrutiny and study and that training needed to be available to help managers develop. He saw management as a much more complex scenario than merely planning the way to improve the output of the business.

Elton Mayo

Mayo was born in Australia in 1880 and then went to spend most of his working life in the United States. Mayo was one of the leading proponents of the human relations approach to the study of an organization. He became most famous for the Hawthorne Experiments, which were carried out in the General Electrical Company in Chicago in the mid-1920s.

At the time of these experiments, GEC was experiencing many tensions and problems within the organization, and levels of production were falling. It was believed just prior to the experiments that there were many inefficiencies across the company, and that the working environment itself should be substantially improved.

Mayo selected two groups of people and in one *control group* the working environment remained unchanged throughout the experiment. In the other the physical working environment was modified and the resultant shift in productivity noted. The results were confusing because alterations in the physical working environment were modified several times, with some changes being for the better and others for the worse, and throughout these inconsistent changes levels of output in the *test group* continued to improve. It was therefore quickly concluded that the workers in this test group were influenced other than by environmental factors. They concluded that there was high morale among the test group because they felt important (they had been selected to be part of this research), and a good working relationship between themselves and their supervisor and the social contact and relationship with each other were very positive.

A new view began to evolve around workers needing to be treated as a social group with social needs, and Mayo soon became convinced that what was important was not so much the physical factors but the attitude of employees to their work and to their supervisor or team leader.

Further work was carried out in a bank-wiring operation, involving 14 men assembling telephone equipment. The situation had been that output had been steady, although below company expectations. Within this group it became clear that there were some roles which had more status than others, and that within the group there were two cliques, one formal and the other informal (where the real power was). Levels of productivity were determined by the group's own discipline, and any worker who exceeded it was restrained by the social factors within the group.

The conclusions drawn from this second experiment was that work is a group activity and that the concept of every man working for himself was out-dated. Furthermore, Mayo argued, management would be successful or otherwise depending on how and whether it is accepted by groups throughout the business unit. According to Mayo, individual workers felt that there was a need for recognition and a sense of belonging, and that each individual worker's productivity and effectiveness would be conditioned by social demands that were both external and internal to the workplace. The concept of group collaboration, Mayo believed, does not occur by accident; it should be planned for and developed.

The one overriding conclusion that can be drawn from the Mayo Hawthorne *effect* is that the fact that workers were selected for study and given special attention (visits by management, interviews and so on), *itself* caused the change in attitudes and levels of productivity.

Contingency theory

The contingency theory is essentially a view that argues that the most effective and appropriate way of managing an organization depends upon the particular circumstances of each case. The implication here is that each case will be different and therefore the solution to look for will be different, although a *best way* of organization structure, leadership style and management practices will inevitably exist. Contingency theory is a theory that tries to identify those issues that make each situation unique.

Contingency theory argues that the optimum structure of an organization can and will vary from being formal to informal, having either centralized or de-centralized authority, using functional or regional business units or having an approach of matrix management or project teams. In this context, the *ideal* structure is one that offers the employees the best methods of working to optimum effect and making the maximum contribution towards the organization's overall objectives and that this *ideal* will vary from place to place. The type of factors causing this variation include:

● The size of the organization.

● The geographical spread of the organization.

● The way in which technology impacts upon the organization.

● The type of work being undertaken.

Some authorities, *behaviouralist* writers, argue that the more challenging aspects of work will be done better in an environment of delegating authority, or empowerment, and having a culture that allows participation by employees in the decision making process. In addition, the organizational structure will be influenced by the social views, culture and educational standards of its employees, which are further influenced by the prevailing rate of change that the organization faces. In today's working environment, change appears inevitable, and many decisions have to be made *there and then*. The element of research and development is crucial, and employees need to work in an environment of accepting responsibility (implied or actual) to support the ambition to achieve optimum success.

Lawrence and Lorsch were two leading authorities on the contingency school and they suggested that an efficient organization functioning in a rapidly changing environment will be more differentiated than an efficient organization in a stable environment. Lawrence and Lorsch defined *differentiated* as meaning that the organization will have many different aspects of formality in its structure, a range of leadership styles, several planning functions and alternative ways in which it interacts with the marketplace. They argued that variety is essential to deal with the different circumstances that are evident in different parts of the organization's functions. It therefore follows that these *differentiated organizations* need to make greater efforts to integrate successfully and to pull together and work towards a common cause (i.e., achieving the business objectives).

The contingency perspective on leadership provides the view that the most effective style of leadership depends upon the circumstances in which the manager is working. Fielder was one who suggested there were four crucial factors here:

● The *position power* of the leader.

● The structure of the particular task for which the leader is responsible.

● In reality, the extent to which this responsibility can be defined.

● The relationship between the leader and his or her team.

A *possible* example here is that routine and simple work carried out in a factory environment by unskilled workers *could* be managed in a more authoritarian style. Alternatively, a more complex series of work tasks could require team members to use more skill and initiative, working in an environment with a leader who is prepared to delegate or empower employees to participate in the decision making process.

It seems then that contingency management is an approach to management decision making which suggests that there will never be a generic solution to any particular problem. Rather that the way forward will differ depending upon the different circumstances faced on each occasion.

1.3   Culture

Culture is a very complex area and worthy of many volumes; however, we do have the opportunity to discuss some of the more important principles here. We shall do so by considering the work of Charles Handy, who used the word culture in a particular way to categorize different types of organization. Handy believed that culture related to such issues as where the power source was in an organizational hierarchy, how much an organization depends upon established rules and regulations, and what types of communication channels are in existence, for example.

There are many factors that could influence the type of culture and structure an organization has:

a) *The history of the organization* – whether there is centralized ownership (implying a power culture), a more defused type of ownership, or whether the organization is family based.

b) *Size of the organization.* Handy believed that this factor was crucial, and argued that larger organizations would tend to be more formalized. Furthermore, larger organizations, primarily because of their size, would need to have smaller more functional and specialized areas which in themselves would require organization and coordination.

c) *The technology available* – in today's world, this is a very important dimension because technology is very costly and changing very rapidly. There is a tendency towards automation and high investment in technology.

d) *The goals and objectives of an organization.* How an organization establishes what its objectives are is very important, as also is how the organization goes about achieving these objectives. The realities of the achievement of these objectives, and the *real world constraints* that are faced by the organization, are important influences. The way in which the organization pursues these objectives, how the *risk versus reward* equation is balanced, and the availability of resources are important.

e) *The environment in which the organization operates* is important as are the people employed by the organization in determining the type of culture that is evident.

Handy argued that there were four types of culture, each of which implied a slightly different set of *norms* or values – these *norms* (or values), according to Handy, would vary between each organization, and possibly within one organization itself.

We shall consider each type of culture identified by Handy in turn.

Power culture

The power culture identified by Handy usually exists in smaller organizations, possibly trade unions, and is dependent upon a central power source. This central power source can spread influence throughout the organization, and as a result the whole organization is dominated by this central power source. All activities are based on what is expected from the central source, although rules and regulations are rare, and there is little evidence of bureaucratic control. In a power culture, control is exercised by individuals in key positions who are influenced by what comes from the centre and directed by fairly frequent meetings with the central source. Any political decisions that are taken are taken on the need to retain the balance of influence, rather than any logical or procedural approach.

This power culture can be illustrated in the form of a *spider's web* effect, as below:

Figure 1.1: Spider's web

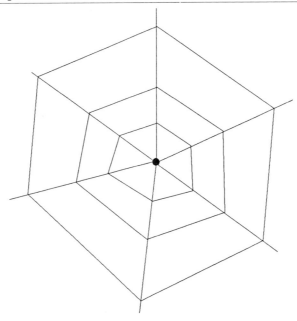

Because this type of organization is small, it has the ability to move quickly and respond promptly – clearly, the way the organization responds, either in the right or wrong way, depends upon the person at the centre of the web. By implication the quality of leadership in a culture like this is crucial to the way in which the organization is run and to the type of power culture that exists.

In a power culture the key aspects of power are shared between the individuals at the centre, and those in key positions, as mentioned above. All of these individuals are likely to be power focused, and politically aware and motivated – it may be that the size of the *web* will continue to grow and possibly even span other organizations, or their *webs*. The central control ensures that the balance between giving independence to key individuals and retaining ultimate control is kept, usually by keeping absolute control on all aspects of finance.

In a power culture, success is judged by results only and focuses heavily on the delivery of targets.

Role culture

This type of culture, according to Handy, works by rationality and logic. The organization itself is dependent upon its various functions which have their own areas of strength and influence. Examples of such functions are, production, human resources, purchasing, supply, and so on.

This type of culture can be illustrated as over the page (the Greek temple):

Figure 1.2: Greek temple

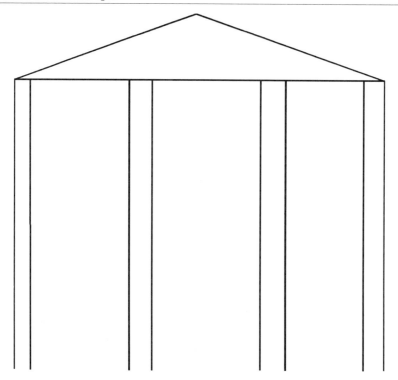

Links between the various functions and the top of the organization are by procedural dimensions, the way in which the communication system works, and possibly the way in which any disputes or debates are settled. All these various aspects are coordinated by the *top management*.

In the role culture environment, the individuals are selected for particular roles on the basis of their ability to complete that particular function to that required level, and probably no more – overachievement is not actively pursued, according to Handy, in this type of culture. In fact, exceeding personal targets or objectives can be seen as disruptive in this type of environment.

A role culture is successful in a stable environment, and probably where the organization itself can control its environment by being in a monopolistic or oligopolistic position in the marketplace – by implication this type of marketplace is more predictable or controlled. Examples of successful role culture include the civil service, oil companies and some retail banks.

Handy argued that this type of culture offers the greatest degree of job security and stability to its employees – historically, promotion can be anticipated, and that rewards and recognition are available to all employees who do what they are asked. A role culture can be found where economies of scale are very important and where specific areas of expertise are crucial to the function of the organization and are seen as a priority over being innovative or cost focused.

Task culture

Handy believed that the task culture is one that is more job or project focused and can be illustrated in the form of a *matrix*, as below:

Figure 1.3: Matrix

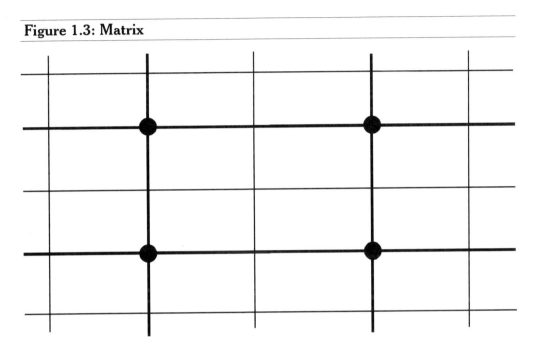

You will see from the diagram that some of the lines in this matrix are thicker and more pronounced, and the key sources of power usually lie where these thicker dimensions meet.

In this type of environment most influence is based on having expert power (i.e., the appropriate skill and knowledge) rather than on position or personal power. The aspect of team culture is also very important and delivery of results through the team is a priority, and takes higher importance than the achievement of individuals and the status of individuals within that team. As a result, influence is very widely spread throughout the organization, and each person within all of the teams should have a feeling that they can contribute, and then actively do contribute to the success of the organization. One of the main themes of a task culture that it is able to maximize the contribution that the whole array of employees can make to business performance.

By its very nature, a task culture needs to be adaptable, responsive, and able to change very quickly, and often towards different directions. This of course is implied by the type of activities that the task culture would be involved in, and project activities.

Handy believed that the task culture are very evident in marketing departments, consultancies, and advertising agencies.

In a task culture the exercise of control from the *top* of the organization can prove difficult – the reason for this is that while ultimate control is retained by top management (for example, the project manager, the head of the task force), in practice only limited control can be exercised from the *top* unless the cultures *norms* are violated. This type of culture has much emphasis on team or group performance, and emphasizing the need to deliver results through people.

Person culture

In this type of organization, each individual is a centre point of the organization and the whole organization exists to serve each individual who works within it. There is a minimal emphasis on structure, and within a larger organization any individuals who group together, say to form a team, in fact evolve to their own personal culture. Clearly in reality, very few organizations can exist and survive with a culture like this – the primary reason being that organizations have overall objectives and need to achieve business results, and these take inevitable precedence over those individual objectives of each employee.

A person culture can be illustrated below (the Galaxy diagram):

Figure 1.4: Galaxy diagram

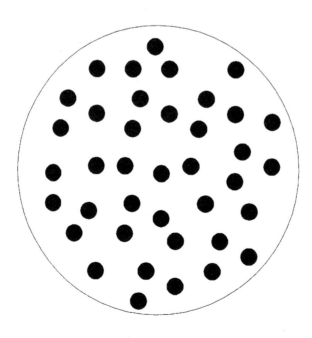

In a person culture, Handy believed that any type of control mechanism managerial hierarchy is impossible unless there is total agreement for any arrangement of this type. In this type of environment, the organization is totally dependent upon the individual.

The type of environment which comes nearest to a person culture is a commune, a cooperative, or a kibbutz, although even in this type of environment, the *organizational* aspect may soon start to create its own identity and inevitably begin to influence individuals themselves. Other possibilities where a person culture may exist could be in a barrister's chamber, a social group or possibly a consultancy firm.

1.4   Communication

Communication as a management skill is discussed elsewhere, and what we shall be trying to establish here are some of the fundamental principles of communication.

The first of these principles is that communication should always add value. This means that each of us should always consider the decisions or plans, for example, the *receivers* of any communication will make as a result of the communication itself. Basic questions to ask ourselves beforehand, therefore, include *what am I trying to achieve by this communication?* and *is this presentation, meeting or discussion (for example) really necessary?* So already, we have seen that communication is not just about keeping people informed or up to date.

The way in which communication is managed is a very important factor. It is obviously not enough for a manager or team leader merely to have an *open door* policy. A manager or team leader has to actively take an interest in communication within the business unit. Being active in asking questions about how the various aspects of communication are progressing is a good start. For example, discussing with colleagues how meetings they attended actually went and what benefits they derived from attending. Sitting down with these colleagues and de-briefing a meeting that they attended on your behalf is another example.

We also need to be aware that communication is multi-dimensional. To call communication one-way or two-way is far too simplistic. Managers and team leaders need to be aware of these various communication flows which interrelate across all aspects of their business unit.

Most research seems to indicate that communication can be very effective if a particular message is repeated in various different ways. A particular message could be communicated in writing, via a memo and/or poster, confirmed verbally and then discussed in groups later on.

Of the many choices available to us when we communicate, the most popular include:

● Within groups, holding presentations, meetings, or facilitating discussion groups.

● In writing, the use of newsletters, memos, or circulars.

● Using *informal* communication channels, such as, for example, the grapevine. This means specific messages can be spread through the *opinion leaders* who exist within every business unit.

- When a manager or team leader leads by example, and thereby makes the symbolic gestures to endorse a message that has been delivered. Essentially, in this case, a team leader's actions would speak louder than (and endorse) words (and other forms of communication).

We have mentioned that communication is much more than a one-way *cascade*. It is usually much more effective if everybody within the business unit feels some *ownership* for any aspect of communication. Quite often, team members welcome the chance to voice their opinions, and have the chance to talk to each other and ask any questions or clarify any issues that may be causing confusion. In addition, by involving team members throughout, they have the opportunity to contribute their own ideas to any communication initiative.

In every business unit, all unit heads need to avoid creating a *blame culture*. Ultimately, this situation means that individuals within that business unit are afraid to speak up, voice their honest opinions, question the views of the manager, or make alternative proposals for fear of recrimination or that their own opinions will be held against them. The unit head, therefore, needs to constantly and genuinely invite the opinions of the whole team and create a working environment of trust, openness and honesty.

These days, the skill of communication is vitally important because most people work in organizations that are consistently changing. This means that the manager or team leader has a key responsibility for keeping the whole team informed. Communication takes up a significant amount of a manager's time, and so it is even more important that this time is spent effectively. When possible, the effectiveness of a business unit approach to communication should be evaluated. One way of doing this is to select a particular issue, probably one that the whole team should already know about, or an issue that is currently being communicated. The manager can then chat to individuals on an informal basis just to see how well (or not) communication appears to be working. What you find may surprise you, although in any case the whole process of communication needs to constantly evolve. All effective managers look for continuous ways of improving how communication is carried out within their business unit.

If handled with care, and probably also depending upon the size of your business unit, a communication survey could be organized. Perhaps a member of the team could design a questionnaire to be used, if the manager feels that the questionnaire should not be seen to come *from the top*. Clearly, any survey of this sort needs to be handled with care and again in a working environment of honesty and openness combined with trust. The surveys being completed will be worthless if those that are completing them do not feel able to do so in an honest way. Similarly, if, as is often the case, the manager or team leader is surprised (and possibly shocked!) by the results, he or she should to be seen to learn from and accept the opinions of their team.

It can also help the communication process within a business unit if the team leader meets the team to discuss it. During these meetings, it could be discussed exactly what types of communication and/or information the team leader expects from the team and what communication and/or information the team expects from the team leader. This is another useful way of raising any issues of confusion in terms of communication, identifying any areas that could be improved, and even questioning why one particular aspect of communication is done in the first place.

2

MANAGEMENT SKILLS

2.1   Management theories and processes

The management process

In the first part of this section we shall consider briefly six of the main elements of the management process. Some of these elements will be considered in greater detail elsewhere.

Planning

This is where thought is given to what has to be done and is the devising of processes that are used to determine the ways and means by which objectives can be achieved.

Effective planning has the following features:

- Obtaining knowledge of all the facts and circumstances surrounding any given situation.

- Planning should be evident at all levels of management.

- The planning that takes place at the *higher levels* will determine the objectives for the planning at *lower levels* of an organization.

- The ultimate achievement is that overall objectives will be dependent upon more detailed planning at the *lower levels* of an organization.

- Planning must be a continuous and evolving process which will carry an organization forward and will therefore need to be adaptable and flexible in order to accommodate the ongoing environment of rapid change.

- Ultimately, the planning process means that the planner (or decision maker) must make a choice between the available and realistic alternatives.

Organization

This is where resources are deployed in order to achieve any given objective and has the following main features:

- Organization is a means to an end, not an end in itself.

- Effective organization requires the recognition of those activities necessary to achieve any given objective.

- All activities must be prioritized or grouped together in order to achieve maximum return from the resources used.

- Various levels of authority, together with the appropriate spans of control, must be established in order for an organization to be effective throughout a business unit.

Staff management

This is where each unit head, team leader or manager endeavours to get the right people in place to help to achieve the overall objectives. The key features of this approach are as follows:

- Ensuring that all roles are clearly defined by job specification or terms of reference.

- Being fully aware of how effective recruitment and selection policies can help.

- When new members join a team, the importance of how the induction procedures can *add value* must be understood.

- Ongoing training and development must be provided to each member of the team.

Many of these areas of staff management will be discussed elsewhere.

Providing leadership

The basis for effective leadership is largely determined by clearly defined objectives and supported by the organizational strategy itself. Leading a team effectively can be facilitated where members of that team are effectively trained and the working environment is one in which there are excellent lines of multi-directional communication.

Broadly, a good leader needs to concentrate on managing resources and leading effectively which assumes, not only the above, but also that levels of morale are good because ultimately the manager or team leader is also required to give effective direction to the team.

Coordination

This aspect of effective management is where harmony of effort (of a team) is pursued. The main features are:

- Coordination must be *designed into* an organization, in a similar way as as it is built into a machine.

- This process necessitates that everybody is aware of his or her own *span of control*.

- Effective coordination cannot exist where individuals feel isolated, or in practical terms adopt an isolationist approach to their work.

- The whole philosophy of coordination requires effective communication and understanding between various functions, business units, teams and individuals in order that common aims and objectives can be achieved.

- Effective coordination will not be achieved unless the self interests of the employees are harmonized with the interests of the organization.

Examples of employee *self interests* include:

income	)
leisure	) known as corollary factors
career progression	)
job satisfaction.	)

Examples of organizational interests include:

profit	)
quality	) primary factors
growth	)
reputation in the marketplace	)

- Coordination works best in an environment where rivalry is minimized and where it is given continuous focus and attention.

Controlling

This dimension consists of three main factors: Establishing the required standards of performance; and measuring actual performances; comparing actual performance against standard performance and taking the necessary corrective action.

Where any one of these factors is missing no effective control can exist.

In addition:

- Effective control techniques are designed to ensure whether actual events conform to plan.

- Most control techniques are aimed at influencing positively the performance of the people responsible to the team leader or manager.

In this section we shall now go on to consider some views and opinions as to how these various aspects of effective management work in practice.

Rensis Likert – new patterns of management

Most research over recent years has shown very clearly that both managers and team leaders who achieve consistently better performance (for example, greater productivity, higher earnings, lower costs) differ significantly in their leadership principles and practices from those achieving poorer performances. For most, this variation is seen to reflect critical differences in basic assumptions about ways of managing people. One of the early thinkers in this respect was Likert who forwarded some leadership principles and practices which, he claimed, would lead to better performance and called *employee-centred supervision*.

Likert called on managers and team leaders to focus their primary attention on the human aspects of their team member's problems and on endeavouring to build effective working groups with high performance goals, *employee centres*. Alternatively, Likert was clearly aware of previous management theories and studies which had been based upon work simplification and the de-skilling of labour, where conformity was seen as very important, where specified tasks were undertaken in a specified way and wherever possible reward was directly linked to output (for example, the earlier views of Fayol and Taylor). Likert called this type of approach *job-centred*. By implication Likert anticipated these *job-centred* managers and team leaders more likely to be in charge of business units that had lower rather than higher levels of productivity and activity.

Likert put forward five main conditions for what he saw to be effective supervisory behaviour:

The principle of supportive relations

The leadership and other main processes of any organization must exist to assure that every manager or team leader, in the context of their interaction within the organization, has the maximum opportunity to be seen as supportive, and to build and maintain the sense of personal worth and importance of each member of each team throughout the business.

Group methods of supervision

Management can make full use of the potential capacity of its human resources only when each person in an organization is a member of one or more effectively functioning work groups or teams that have a high degree of:

● Group loyalty

● Effective skills of interaction

● High performance goals

High performance goals

If a high level of performance is to be achieved, Likert argued that it is necessary for a manager or team leader to be *employee-centred*, and at the same time to have high performance goals and a contagious enthusiasm as to the importance of achieving these goals.

Technical knowledge

The effective leader has adequate competence to handle the technical problems faced by the group or team, or ensures that access to this technical knowledge is fully available.

Coordinating, scheduling, planning

The effective leader, according to Likert, must fully reflect and effectively represent the views, goals, values and decisions of the group or team in those other groups where the manager or team leader liaises between his or her own group and the rest of the organization. In addition, a manager or team leader must bring to his or her own group the views, goals, and decisions of those other groups with which they are involved. This approach provides the vehicle whereby communication and the exercise of influence can be performed in both directions.

Short-term and long-term results

Likert also believed that there is a temptation for many managers and team leaders to adopt the highly authoritarian *job-centred* style, and indeed this *may* show higher performance in the short term. In today's world, many such manager's and team leader's results are reviewed and incentivized on short-term results and any case (even in today's flatter *job market*), many managers may expect to be transferred to develop their own careers after only a few years (still relatively short term).

The longer-term implications of this *job-centred* style are that greater costs may be required for remedial and quality control measures, increased absence rates and staff turnover may occur and possibly even increased level of staff grievances and disputes. All of these possible long-term implications will affect the ongoing performance of the organization, but are not always associated with the (inappropriate) style of leadership.

These longer-term implications which result from the short-term, apparently more attractive, job-centred styles, Likert suggests, should be recognized as effectively liquidating any organizational investment in human resources. In simple terms *improved output* cannot be attained and maintained if the assets in human resources are being *run down* – conventional accounting data tends to ignore the value of human assets (for example, high levels of motivation, willingness to adapt and face change, good communication, and so on), but there is no doubt that they do exist.

John Adair – Action centred-leadership

John Adair saw the leader's responsibilities falling into three categories:

- Achieving the task.
- Building the team.
- Satisfying individual needs.

Essentially then any leader must try to achieve *a balance* by acting in all three areas in their relative importance for the particular situation that is faced. Clearly, in some circumstances greater focus must be given to achieving a task, and on other occasions to satisfy an individual need. The clear message here is that each of these three aspects needs to be thought about and acted upon in the appropriate proportion, depending upon the particulars of any given set of circumstances.

Task need

Organizations and business units have a task: to make a profit, provide a service, achieve survival. So anyone who manages others has to achieve results: through production, marketing, selling or whatever. Therefore, achieving objectives, or achieving the task, is a major criterion of success. Further, the difference between a team and a random crowd is that a team has some common purpose, goal or objective – if a work team does not achieve the required results or a meaningful result then frustration occurs; an effective team leader has to guide the team towards achieving its objectives.

Team needs

To achieve its tasks or business objectives, a group needs to be held together. The team has to be working in a coordinated fashion with all its members pulling in the same direction, and this develops the philosophy that effective teamwork will ensure that the team's collective contribution will be greater than the sum of its (individual) parts. Any conflict that arises within the team must be used effectively, arguments can generate discussions that lead to ideas and a positive way forward or alternatively can lead to tension, diverseness and a lack of cooperation.

Individual needs

Within any working team or group each individual has his or her own set of needs. Individual members need to know and understand what their responsibilities are, how they will *add value* to their team's performance, and to receive regular feedback on their performance. In addition, each individual should have the opportunity to show full potential, and to develop, to take on responsibility and to receive recognition, encouragement and positive feedback for good work.

With Adair's three-dimensional model, this can be illustrated as over the page:

Figure 2.1: Adair's three-dimensional model

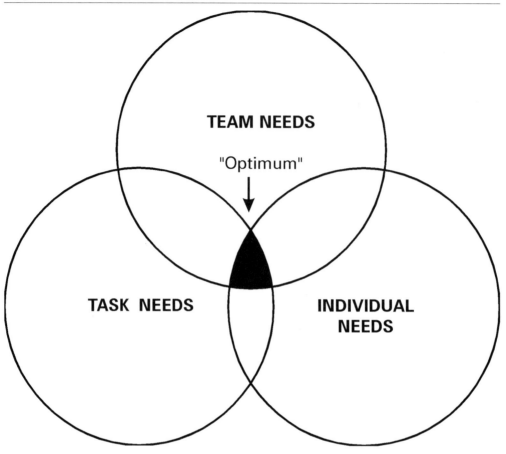

This is Adair's model in graphical terms; the table on the opposite page shows how particular managerial functions can impact on the task, team and individual needs:

Adair's leadership check list

Function	Task	Team	Individual Needs (Own and Team)
Define Objectives	Identify task, clarify objectives and constraints.	Discuss, agree and set targets. Involve the team throughout.	Discuss, agree and set targets. Define responsibilities, objectives and priorities.
Plan	Establish resources priorities. Discuss and decide what needs to happen, by when, who is involved.	Structure and delegate. Agree roles and responsibilities.	Assess skills of individuals. Train. Delegate.
Communicate	Brief and regularly check understanding. Ensure good communication channels are in place and are effective.	Regularly consult and obtain feedback from the team.	Listen) Walk Advise) the Enthuse) job
Support/Control	Regularly monitor. Discuss, agree, regularly review and check standards.	Coordinate activities. Reconcile differences. Manage conflict.	Recognize success. Encourage good performance. Counsel.
Evaluate	Ongoing process. Replan as necessary. Summarize and communicate any any changes.	Reward success. Learn from success and failure.	Appraise and guide. Concept of continuous improvement.

Management by objectives

Management by objectives (MBO) is a system of management that can be seen to incorporate much of Douglas McGregor's Theory "Y", much of Herzberg's work on the value of *satisfiers* as opposed to *hygiene* factors, and many of the current views on key managerial attributes like delegation, communication and coordination.

MBO was devised by John Humble and is defined as "a dynamic system which seeks to integrate the company's need to clarify and achieve its profit and growth goals with a manager's need to contribute to these goals and develop himself or herself".

At the outset, MBO requires a definition of an organization's aims and objectives, and an acceptance in reality by managers at all levels that they must share in the setting of company objectives and standards, and in all achievement of these objectives and standards, themselves. In other words MBO depends on effective teamwork if it is to be operated successfully, and in the course of this operation it further develops team work.

The first and sometimes most difficult problem with an MBO system is the definition of the organizational objectives. This part of the process will involve asking following fundamental questions about the organization:

- What business are we in?
- What are the growth areas and what are the decline areas of our business?
- What image do we have now and what image do we want?
- What actions are necessary in order that we should not fall behind our competitors?
- Where do we wish to be x years from now?

Clearly, these are basic policy making decisions and one of the most important advantages of MBO is that it forces senior management to face up to these issues.

Once the organizational objectives have been defined the next stage is to arrive at the, say, regional, area, or more local business unit objectives – which of these comes first and how they interrelate with each other will depend upon what sort of organization is being considered. From the second-stage objectives you will derive the third- and fourth-level, more sectional and local, objectives.

For any given manager, whether senior executive, regional or more local, some objectives will be more crucial to success than others and this is the rationale behind the selection of key result areas or of critical accountability areas or particular emphasis in the MBO system. Almost by definition, it is generally true to say that managers do concentrate most on short-term objectives anyway and it is often the more longer-term, less easily measured aspects of their responsibilities upon which they need to be encouraged to devote more thought. For this reason, the key results area concept needs to be kept in perspective; otherwise it could be a major influence in reducing the overall efficiency of senior and middle management.

Under MBO, at a previously agreed interval (possibly every three months), the performances of the middle and more junior managers are appraised by more senior managers. Ideally, the key results areas are examined one by one and separately from the other areas. This process of key results analysis is meant to enable objective measurement to be introduced into the process of assessing results. The MBO approach determines that this appraisal should not be considered as opportunity for criticism; it should be seen as a way of assessing the realism of the objectives and the effectiveness of the manager concerned. This stage of the process is also more than just a merit-rating since the appraisal does not simply examine certain character traits and performance indexes. It now should be seen as a way of measuring performance against clearly prescribed, and previously agreed, standards.

To achieve maximum impact and effect, the periodic appraisals should be supported by a regular and ongoing monitoring of results, which will mean that consultation and action will not only take place in times of crisis. Not only will monitoring enable warnings to be seen in good time, so that they may be reviewed before they become critical, this approach will also enable the *appraisers* to catch one of their team doing something well!

From what we have seen already, the system of MBO cannot be introduced and in any case could not be introduced successfully without considerable thought and planning beforehand. Some of the major steps in this process can be identified as follows:

1) Carrying out a management audit which involves defining the management structure from top to bottom, and showing levels of authority, spans of management and functional relationships by means of an organization chart. By doing this senior management will be able to see the involvement of all people within the organizational structure and how they will fit in to the proposed system of MBO, and be able also to demonstrate potential managerial cover or all areas of responsibility. By then comparing the existing organization with what is required will identify the strengths and weaknesses in the structure. An audit like this is also a valuable aid in any subsequent exercises in manpower or succession planning.

2) There then should be a review of control systems and procedures. These supporting procedures are essential, because they will provide management information which will be depended upon. If these sub-systems are inadequate neither MBO or any other system of management can function to its full potential.

3) The next step is an analysis of managerial jobs as to size, purpose and scope. This is an essential preparation to the objective- and target-setting part of MBO which will also help to identify the key results areas.

4) Here there is a review of the communication systems throughout the organization. Good multi-directional communication systems are essential if each level of managers is to know its objectives and to have played a part in discussing and agreeing them. In addition, each manager should know how his or her own objectives form part of the wider organization's objectives. In reality, the lower down the company's organization, the more difficult it may be for managers or team leaders to discuss and agree their expected performance. Sometimes more junior managers will expect to receive directives rather than to have to debate objectives and how to achieve them. Also, some senior managers may find it difficult in the face of other pressures to become involved in setting subordinate managers or team leaders task and priority objectives. In any case, the communication process has to be thorough to avoid misunderstanding, frustration and possible failure, in this case in trying to set up an MBO system.

5) Prior to MBO being introduced all individuals within an organization should be well prepared. Most managers will require training before the introduction of MBO because:

- They may seek to minimize the risk.

- Most managers without guidance may seek to minimize the risk of failure by setting targets which are very easily attainable.

- MBO implies that managers will rely more upon themselves and on their teams rather than on their superiors. In a way, then, MBO is one way of ensuring delegation, since it sets out to involve managers in decision making at the highest level of which they are capable. This attitude needs ongoing training and support, together with a culture that encourages self development.

- MBO seeks to exploit a person's potential to the full, and again ongoing training and support will facilitate this aim.

Benefits of MBO

The main benefits an organization would hope to gain from successful MBO are as follows:

- An explicit, kept up to date, statement of the company's aims and objectives.

- A plan for the achievement of those aims and objectives based upon the contribution required of each member of the management team.

- An adequate system of management information systems which provide the data necessary for effective management.

- A system of multi-directional communication which ensures that effective action will be taken where necessary.

- The understanding and acceptance of all members of the team of their role and of how they can personally contribute to the success of the organization.

- A method of identifying these strengths and weaknesses of the management team and thereby identifying guidance for future training and development.

2.2   Planning

Owen and Arkwright were among the earliest thinkers in considering planning as a management process, relating to factory layouts. Their principles were to emphasize the orderliness of the workflow and factory cleanliness. Even in those early days, factory technology demanded the planning of power sources and connections, the arrangement of machinery and space for a smooth flow of work and the reduction of confusion through well-placed stores of materials and access to them.

Over time, planning assumed a new importance for the entrepreneur, a manager or team leader. In its crudest form this meant:

- Organizations required ongoing, sometimes significant, investments, which need to be planned for.

- Workflows had to be arranged to meet the needs of an ever-changing business environment.

- Human resources had to be recruited and trained to meet the demands of the business.

Taylor in his work separated the roles of planning and doing. His concept of the *functional foreman* were designed to bring expert knowledge to bear upon production scheduling, workflows and production control.

Fayol identified planning and forecasting as the first steps in the process of managerial actions and wrote of the need for *unity of direction* in plans and in leadership. The management process approach which emerged from the pioneering work of Fayol based the planning concept on a broader plain and not just only on production. Planning became almost synonymous with decision making and was intended to incorporate all business activities and not just production.

The 1960s saw a watershed in views on planning process and it assumed new dimensions due to:

- The growth of automated factories.

- The advent of high technology.

In recent years, and projecting to the future, knowledge of the planning function has vastly increased, and as a result, has a primary function to maximize the efficient utilization of physical resources with a focus on enhancing the satisfaction of the human resource.

2.3   Control

Control is the management activity that detects changes or deviations from those originally planned. Examples of such control systems include: quality control, budgetary control and stock control. Clearly, effective management information is essential to enable effective control activities to take place. Control is, therefore, not an end in itself; it is merely a way in which to continually improve an existing system.

Within any control system the element of feedback is crucial because without this dimension it will be impossible to assess *actual performance* against *planned performance* and make the necessary amendments.

A control system can be illustrated as over the page:

Figure 2.2: Control system

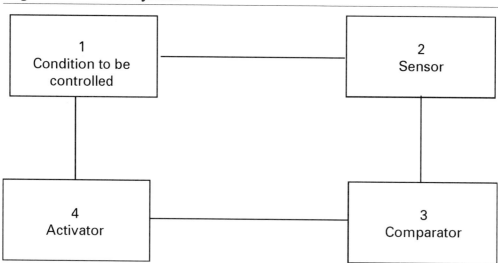

Looking at each aspect of the above diagram in turn:

Condition to be controlled

This aspect is the output from the system itself or the system against which the control element is being applied to.

Sensor

This is the element of control, how in fact performance is measured.

Comparator

This aspect of the model is the *normal standard* against which levels of performance can be compared. Any deviation from the *norm* is where elements of control can be applied. Any deviation from the *norm* may mean that action takes place or alternatively the *norm* itself may be reviewed.

Activator

This aspect is the part of the business unit that responds to what has happened at the comparator stage. It is where responsibility lies for any corrective action to be taken in the context of:

● The accuracy of the information that has been received (i.e., the feedback).

● How significant is any variation from the current normal standard.

● What, if any, action is now required to restore the system to its former level.

Overall control is maintained through, hopefully, effective information flows. When information is not being readily fed back (to the activator) the control mechanism has no value. Essentially, effective control is exercised by using complete and reliable information.

Closed or open loop systems

What follows are some definitions of different types of systems:

Closed loop – this is where a system exists in which part of the output is fed back to the input so that the system output can affect its input (or some other aspect of this operation).

Closed system – this is a system that does not take in or give out anything to its environment (very rare in practice).

Open loop – this is a type of system in which corrective action is not automatic, but is dependent upon external intervention. Ultimately any control actions are made without reference to the current output of the system.

Open system – this is a system that is connected to and interacts with its environment.

We have already seen that the element of *feedback* is a critical factor in control systems. Feedback systems are often called *closed-loop* systems. Systems without feedback mechanisms in place are called *open-loop* systems. An example of a closed-loop system is in a science laboratory, where physical and chemical reactions occur, and experiments are isolated from their environment. A biological system can be seen as a good example of an open system where external influence (for example, solar energy) and materials are converted into output (for example, growing crops).

2.4   Objective setting

Most of us working today are largely influenced by targets we have to achieve or objectives that have been set for us to focus day-to-day working activities upon. Some of us are in the unfortunate, but often realistic, position of being told what our objectives are going to be. Obviously, a more sensible and motivating way of ensuring that team members feel committed to achieving their objectives is to involve them in the process. This means sitting down with them and discussing what it is we think they can achieve and essentially what they will find motivating, demanding, very challenging, although ultimately (hopefully) achievable. All of us know that unit heads, managers and team leaders have a series of targets they need to meet for their own managers. This ultimately means that their responsibilities must be shared out among their team. Nevertheless it is still absolutely necessary to try to involve a team in the whole process so that at least they feel some degree of ownership and commitment to what it is the business unit is trying to achieve. Each of your team members will be realistic enough to know that they are going to have challenges to meet in the months ahead, and only the most naive would expect these to be easy.

For the vast majority, therefore, it will come as no surprise when the overall team objectives become known, neither will it come as a surprise to them that they will have responsibility for achieving part of these. Simply, it is just best managerial practice to sit down with each of your team members and explain how the whole process will work, how each individual team member will be involved, what it is that you as team leader expect them to achieve, and for them to have their own say about how they feel about the whole process and their involvement within it.

Setting objectives then is partly about sitting down with your team members and discussing mutual roles and expectations. It is more than agreeing a set of targets which are then committed to paper; these objectives are an understanding between two or more people which will govern performance in the months ahead and which will undoubtedly need reviewing on a regular basis. These reviews mean that the manager and each individual team member will sit down and regularly discuss performance against these objectives and gain an understanding as to why some objectives are being met or exceeded, and why, possibly, some objectives are not yet being achieved. In addition, the business world is operating in an environment of rapid change, which means an individual's own objectives may need to change. These changes can be incorporated into part of the regular review process.

These objective-setting meetings and objective review meetings should be planned and organized in advance. They are important events and will involve an investment of time for both the manager, team leader and individual team members. It is worth investing this time because not only are these meetings important, it is vital that no misunderstanding is allowed to creep in about what it is that needs to be done to achieve objectives.

Agreeing effective objectives

An effective objective needs to have several features which we shall identify below using a mnemonic, *SMART*.

Specific

This means that any objective agreed between manager and team member must be precise. Every objective must say specifically what it is an individual is meant to do. For example, to increase weekly sales figures from 10 to 12 insurance policies.

Measurable

Each agreed objective must contain details of how a particular aspect of performance will be appraised or measured. There are four main ways in which these measures may be included:

- Quantity
- Time
- Cost
- Quality

Each objective then should be involving at least one of these categories so that both manager and individual are clear about how their performance will be measured.

Acceptable

As we have discussed above, all objectives should be discussed between the manager and the individual concerned. Ultimately an agreement should be reached between the various parties, and preferably not imposed by one or the other. Strictly this latter approach becomes a process of target setting.

Realistic

All the objectives agreed between the various parties must be something to be strived for, something that is ultimately achievable. There is no point whatsoever in agreeing a series of objectives with team members if they are going to be impossible to achieve. There may be circumstances in which an objective will contain details about what specific circumstances may make achieving that particular objective impossible. Ideally then all parties must be clear that the objectives will be very stretching, would look to gain maximum performance from each individual while being ultimately something that can be achieved.

Time

Each agreed objective must contain details of how long would be appropriate for the achievement of an outcome of a particular objective. Usually this takes the form of a date for completion or an allocation of an amount of time to complete a particular objective.

2.5 Negotiation skills

Negotiation is a very important management skill and it is often a way to move things forward between two sides, and is definitely preferable to confrontation.

Negotiation can be seen to have the following elements:

- The two parties involved in a negotiation process have different interests.

- These two parties are involved in discussions on their differences.

- Eventually these two parties are both prepared to move away from the first stated position towards each other.

We shall consider the various stages of the negotiation process.

Preparation

This is a very important stage, and the following issues need to be considered:

- What your objectives and what the other person's objectives are likely to be.

- What your own priority objectives and the other person's priority objectives are likely to be.

- What approach to the negotiation process you are going to take, and what approach the other person is likely to take.

- What sanctions and/or concessions you are prepared to give and, concurrently, what sanctions or concessions you think the other person may be prepared to give.

- Both parties during the negotiation process should establish very early on what levels of authority each has to agree to particular sanctions or concessions.

- What (if any) common ground can you establish either beforehand or very early on in the negotiation process.

Essentially, both parties to the negotiation process will have a preferred position which can be categorized as follows:

- Objectives that must be achieved in the process.

- Objectives that are intended to be achieved.

- Objectives that it would be nice to achieve.

As the process unfolds, each party to the process will confirm bottom-line objectives and hopefully a degree of overlap is either sought for or achieved with the other side. Ultimately, unless there is such an overlap, the negotiation process cannot begin.

Arguing

At this stage in the negotiation process it is important to ensure that the other party understands your position and is very clear about what it is you are looking to achieve.

At this stage it is very important that you avoid interrupting, trying to score points, blaming the other person, trying to be too clear, being sarcastic or talking too much.

Examples of *best practice* at this *arguing* stage are:

- Listening skills.

- Seeking clarification.

- Regularly summarizing progress.

- Probably being non-committal about the other person's proposals.

- Frequently testing the other person's commitment to his or her various statements and position.

Signalling

During this stage of the negotiation process each party is looking to see what types of indications the other has given towards moving the process forward. For example, which signs of movement have you indicated, or has the other person indicated? Against these signs of movement by either yourself or the other person involved, what sort of responses have been given either by yourself or by the other person? If necessary, perhaps either you or the other person will need to repeat these signals.

Possibly here, there may be no response from the other person, which means that an adjournment in the process may be necessary. Alternatively, either you or the other person in the process may need to revise their position. At this stage both sides should be looking to respond (positively if possible) and reciprocate – both sides should be prepared to listen and recognize any signals given.

Proposing

At this stage of the negotiation process it becomes important that propositions from one side to the other are visible and available – without doubt propositions beat arguments, and arguments cannot be negotiated. Propositions should lead ultimately to solutions and ways forward.

Both sides need to be aware of what is being proposed by the other, and both sides need to be firm on generalities and flexible on specifics. Both sides need to be stating their preferred conditions and be as specific as possible.

Ideally, both sides should be prepared to propose solutions in an open and realistic way rather than be negative.

Packaging

At this stage in the negotiation process both your and the other person's objectives should be clear and agreed in some sort of priority order. Both sides should be aware of the other's signal of possibilities of concessions.

During this stage of the process it makes sense to review both of the party's objectives and to ensure that it is clearly established that:

- Each side has moved towards the other.
- Both sides are clear about what concessions are being given.
- What room for negotiation either party in the process now has.
- Is some sort of parity for both sides now available?
- Have both sides in the process considered all of the alternatives?

Closing and agreeing

Obviously at this stage both sides in the process will have made it very clear what their *bottom lines* are. At this stage both sides need to agree how the negotiation process is to be *closed*.

Obviously both sides should be very clear about what has been agreed, and if necessary understanding should be checked again between both sides to ensure that each interprets the agreements made in exactly the same way.

As with other management skills, negotiation is one that requires some experience and practice, often supported by training. I have tried to outline some of the key parts in the negotiation process although I am sure you will have realized that in reality to try to strictly segment each stage of the process is both naive and impossible. There are undoubted areas of overlap and the way in which each aspect of the process is applied depends upon the type of issue being addressed.

2.6   Delegation

Delegation is one of the main aspects of management to facilitate getting things done through others. In fact, the skill of delegation is one that many managers find difficulty in applying, although many see that the ability to delegate effectively may actually offer some help and support.

We need to be very clear about what we mean when we talk about delegation. Delegation is in no way abdication. Delegation is more about empowering team members, and motivating colleagues, and when *given* the delegator *will always* retain ultimate responsibility for each task that is delegated. This means that the ability to delegate is a key responsibility for every manager or team leader.

Reasons to delegate

Most of us will have the opportunity to delegate particular tasks, and whether this is possible can be partly at least influenced by the following:

- Is there somebody in your team who can do the task better than you can? Delegation enables you to *tap in* to the abilities and expertise of each of your team. Some managers will be reluctant to delegate for this very reason, that is fear, and feeling uncomfortable that somebody else within their team (particularly a subordinate) can complete a task or responsibility better than they can.

- It may be that somebody in your team has more capacity or resource to be able to complete a particular task or function. They may complete this particular responsibility in a way different from what has been the case so far, or from the way that you personally have done it for a period of time. This situation should not negate the possibility of delegation. Just because a member of your team will take on a responsibility and carry it out in a different way, this new way may be more effective than the former methods.

- It may be more cost effective to delegate, because some tasks can be carried out to the level required by a team member rather than a team leader. It obviously makes sense to have the various roles and responsibilities of a team carried out at the right and most cost-effective levels.

- The need to delegate will be heavily influenced by when a task needs to be completed. It may be that you have just too much to do *today*, and that some of these immediate and urgent priorities could be shared around your team. Possibly, through a discussion and agreed re-prioritization of their own tasks, one of your team could take on one of your urgent priorities and provide support in that way.

- Delegation can be used to develop one of your team members. By sharing your own roles and responsibilities, it is almost inevitable that one of your team would personally benefit from doing one of *your* tasks.

The process of delegation

Delegation is a two-way process involving both the delegator (usually the manager or team leader) and the delegatee (the person who is having the responsibility given to them).

Best practice delegation means:

- Both delegator and delegatee are in agreement about what is involved (there is a need to be specific here).

- Both parties are clear as to the desired outcome from this delegation.

- It should be agreed how the performance of the delegatee will be monitored, measured, regularly reviewed and ultimately assessed.

- The timescales involved should be realistic and agreed.

- The appropriate level of authority should be clarified for the delegatee. We have already mentioned that ultimate responsibility for the task completion will always rest with the delegator; however, the delegatee needs to have the appropriate boundaries of authority in order to be able to complete the delegated task unhindered.

The ability to delegate, as with all management skills, requires practice, and most managers and team leaders will become effective delegators over time. Above we have seen some of the generic issues that need to be considered prior to delegating a task. It is not always as easy as this because your team will not consist of identical people with similar skills and abilities. Therefore, there are some additional areas that should be considered as we gain our experience in the skill of delegation:

- For each task that is to be delegated, consider who from your team is the most appropriate person to delegate to. Important factors here are peoples' abilities (actual or potential), their attitude to their duties, their existing workload, your plans for them for the future.

- Perhaps share the possibility of delegating a task with your team members and see what they think about having the task delegated to them. This has the dual benefit of involving your whole team in the process, before deciding who you will allocate the specific task or tasks to.

- Delegation should be a proactive activity rather than a series of reactive and crisis management issues. This means that the ability to delegate effectively is closely linked to the ability to plan for the future. With a clearer picture of the short-, medium- and longer-term priorities (accepting fully that in today's world these priorities may well change), it becomes possible to plan your delegation in advance. This gives the delegator and delegatee much   more time to prepare for, plan and implement the tasks for which they have responsibility.

- When it is realistic to do so, the delegator should try to delegate *whole* tasks to the delegatee. As a result, the delegatee has the implied authority to carry out a whole part of the team leader's or manager's role. Usually, the motivation and empowerment effects of this approach will be far greater than if the delegatee is merely given a small part of a larger task to carry out on the delegator's behalf.

- From the outset, both the delegator and delegatee need to be very clear, in as precise terms as possible, the desired outcomes from this particular delegation. This will mean that the delegatee is very clear from the outset what results are expected by you as delegator on this and each occasion.

- It is very important not to rush the process of delegation. This approach aligns closely to the main implied danger of delegation, namely abdication. It is very important that delegators take the time to consider who should carry out specific tasks on their behalf. In addition, the delegatee's current levels of knowledge, training requirements, appropriate skill levels, ability to take on these additional tasks, levels of experience all need to be closely evaluated. Without this level of understanding about their delegatees, the delegator may delegate the wrong task to the wrong person at the wrong time for the wrong reasons.

- Delegation is not only about sharing out the more glamorous parts of your role. Neither is delegation about *dumping* all the mediocre parts of your role elsewhere. Obviously, a balance needs to be struck between delegating all different aspects of your role, when and if appropriate. At one extreme, it is not always appropriate to keep all the good, stimulating and interesting roles for yourself and thereby lose the opportunity to motivate your team members by delegating parts of these roles to them. At the other extreme, neither do you want to delegate all the key aspects of your role elsewhere and retain all the mundane, more boring, less cost-effective (and even *playpen*) activities for yourself.

- You should be able to completely trust the person to whom you have delegated a task. In the context of the delegator needing to be aware of what the delegatee is up to, and reviewing regularly what is going on and what progress has been made, it is usually best to let the delegatee proceed on his or her own. This approach means that the motivational and empowerment affects can be maximized, as by doing this, the delegatee gets a clear message that you actually trust him or her to deliver a particular task to the required level on your behalf.

2.7   Problem solving and decision making

The decision making process is often made easier if we consider it in its constituent parts. By adopting this approach we can then take each stage at a time, accepting fully that, in reality, each part will interact with each other.

One way of looking at the whole process is to segment it as follows:

- *Recognition* – at this stage we should be aware that there is a problem, or a decision that will eventually have to be made, or the potential for a problem or challenge in the future.

- *Definition* – here we should be looking to define the problem/challenge as specifically and precisely as possible. This will give everybody concerned a clear indication of what it is that needs to be faced and dealt with. If the problem is work-related it usually needs to be defined in terms of impact on the business; for example in terms of costs, time or some other resource.

- *Data collection* – at this stage it is really important to collect and collate as much information on the problem/challenge as possible. It is here that the foundation for the way in which the problem will eventually be dealt with is laid. Here also, when possible, we should be looking for the various causes of and effects of various aspects of the situation we are about to deal with.

- *Analysis* – from the range of data and information that has been collated, it is then appropriate to put all this into some kind of order and priority. The information at your disposal needs to be categorized into important and critical (in terms of this particular problem) as against the less important, and possibly less relevant. On the vast majority of occasions, it will be the fact-based information you have collected that will be much more important and useful than subjective information and opinion.

- *Define your objective* – this definition will give all concerned a clear idea of where you are looking to get to once the problem/challenge has been dealt with. In the same way as when the problem was defined, when looking to where you are looking to get to, a clear definition is also very important. These desired outcomes should be specific, when possible measurable, and ultimately realistically achievable within a defined timescale.

- *Considering the available options* – before deciding the way ahead, it is crucial that the various ways to proceed are considered and thought through. When it is realistic to do so, it is advisable to look for and consider as many alternatives as possible. Sometimes, it is not always the most obvious solutions that are the best, and creative management techniques (for example brain storming) may reveal some more innovate ways of proceeding.

- *Best way forward* – this is where you consider, either yourself or with the involvement of your team, which is the best option to proceed with. Clearly, others opinions will be important, the effect of each option upon everybody else needs to be considered, and the pros/cons of future options need to be debated thoroughly prior to making a decision.

- *Implementation* – this is when the most preferred option has been selected, and now needs to be converted into action. One of the first priorities will be to communicate to all of those who will be involved at this implementation stage that the decision has been made. These days an action plan will follow which will indicate more precisely the various roles and responsibilities, what needs to be delivered by when (and by whom), timescales, and also how progress will be measured and evaluated.

- *Monitoring progress* – with the decision of which options to choose taken, and now being implemented, the months ahead may not all run to plan. This means that any action plan, for example, needs to be adaptable, to accommodate any changes, foreseen or unforeseen, that may arise. Regular reviews of progress will help to establish whether the original plans are progressing as expected, and if so all would appear to be well. If there are any discrepancies, the underlying reasons for these discrepancies should be quickly established, and any remedial action taken and incorporated into a revised plan.

Force field analysis

Any problem or challenge that we face can be described in terms of a balance between two (opposing) sets of forces. One set of forces will be seen as helpful (or positive) and the other set seen as hindering (or negative). Examples of helping forces could be pay and working conditions. An example of a hindering or negative force could be poor supervision.

Sometimes it is easier to illustrate this situation in a visual way, as below:

Figure 2.3: The balance of forces

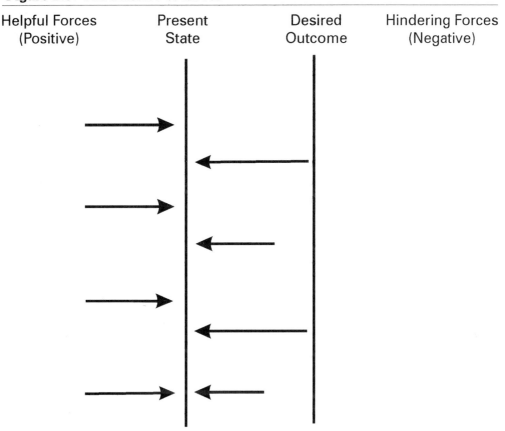

Helpful Forces (Positive)   Present State   Desired Outcome   Hindering Forces (Negative)

In adopting this approach to looking at the problem, clearly the first stage is to identify the helpful and hindering forces. Next, these opposing forces must be *weighted* in terms of the amount of *force* either positively or negatively that they exert. Clearly, this process is not an exact science, although if this analysis involves a group discussion, in the vast majority of situations there will be unanimous opinion about where the major forces lie.

Essentially, changes in the situation can be brought about in two ways:

a) By increasing the impact of the helpful or positive forces.

b) By reducing the impact of the hindering or negative forces.

You will have already grasped that this force field analysis is a very practical process and it is worthwhile outlining the process that you could follow when applying this approach.

● Firstly, select a particular issue that, by spending some time on, will add value to your business unit.

● Define specifically this problem or issue in terms of the present situation, and then exactly how you would like to see this situation change (for the better) in the future.

- Then, when possible with your close colleagues, consider which forces are working in helpful and hindering ways in this particular situation. Examples of forces that could be on either side of the equation include: people, money, time, resources, working conditions, competition in the marketplace, communication – the list is potentially endless. Remember, it is often helpful to consider this approach in diagrammatic form, as illustrated above.

- If you do use a diagram, called a force field diagram, label each of the arrows (remember to put each label in the right section!), with the length of each arrow signifying, as accurately as possible, the strength and impact of each issue. The longer the arrow, the stronger the force either positively or negatively.

- Then consider each hindering force individually and establish what specific actions could be taken to reduce or eliminate this particular force. It is obviously beneficial to discuss actions in specific and realistic terms rather than to waste time debating *blue sky* solutions.

- You can then consider each helping force, and also identify what specific and realistic actions that could be taken to increase the force to have an even more positive impact. Please remember that each individual hindering force or helpful force may not affect the overall problem in isolation. You may therefore need to consider more than one hindering or helpful force at the same time. Similarly, the emphasis you give to particular hindering forces or helping forces will depend on the particulars of each case and exactly what it is that you are looking to achieve as a result of your actions.

- Once the priority hindering forces and helping forces have been established, an action plan will usually evolve. Here, the priority actions that could be taken should be agreed, in point terms, clarifying what you are looking to achieve over a given period of time. Again, what is discussed at this stage needs to be realistic in terms of what is possible and what resources are available to help support your plan of action.

Force field analysis can work particularly well when the hindering and helping forces fall into the category of problems that can be solved or influenced by you and your team. Clearly, the whole process becomes that much more difficult when you are considering the various forces that affect problems over which you and your group have absolutely no control.

2.8   Communication

There are various aspects to communicating effectively and there is no doubt in today's working world communication is a key management skill. We have seen elsewhere some of the issues that need to be considered when communicating across an organization and in this section we shall be concentrating more on communicating on a *one-to-one* basis and considering some of the main aspects of this skill.

Listening skills
The ability to listen does not only mean using your ears. It is a skill that involves a great deal

of concentration, integrating aspects of body language, eye contact, and focused thought. Listening skills are skills that require a great deal of practice and the ultimate check of an effective listener is when you never have to return to somebody to clarify what has already been said.

In a typical working day, all of us spend time at the PC, digesting information, in conversation, and listening to others. We therefore have plenty of time to practise listening to others, and in any case this will help you save time, avoid errors, enhance communication and be seen as someone who everybody wants to communicate with.

On each occasion when listening is involved some options for action include:

● Ask questions, when appropriate to clarify and check understanding.

● Write it down!

● Ensure the communicator understands what he or she means!

● It is all too easy, particularly in a busy working environment (they all are these days!), not to listen effectively. All of us can relate to the scenario that we are looking at someone while they are speaking, while actually thinking of something else, hearing what has been said but not actually listening, not giving the communicator complete attention because you actually disagree with what he or she is saying, or even interrupting. It is essential that on each occasion we try to let the communicator complete what they want to say while we are a listener, try not to formulate a response too early or to look blatantly bored or uninterested. Not only is it best practice in terms of listening skills not to put up these barriers, it is also good manners.

Some ways around these barriers include:

● Think how annoyed you would be if you were interrupted when speaking.

● Always try to keep an open mind.

● Think what the communicator is thinking of you if you are blatantly disinterested.

● Try to concentrate on what is being said now rather than trying to predict what is about to be said.

● Avoid the temptation to interrupt.

● Seek clarity when appropriate.

We must all try to gauge the communicator's body language, to try to understand the feelings of the communicator and listen to his or her tone of voice. This is particularly important because it helps a listener not only to hear what is being said, but also to gain some understanding of the feelings and emotions that the communicator is concurrently relaying.

Questioning skills

Effective questioning techniques are very important aspects of communication skills. Effective questioning can help to facilitate problem solving, and also to check understanding of what is being said.

There are two main types of questions, open questions and closed questions.

An open question typically begins with *why, how, who, what, where*. This means when beginning a question with a word like this you immediately invite a broader and more detailed response, and sometimes find out more about an issue than the other person has actually said.

A closed question is much more direct, one where a *yes or no* answer is usually called for.

There will be occasions when conversations focus on mostly *open* questions, and others when more *closed* questions are appropriate. Probably many of our day-to-day conversations typically involve a balance between these two types of questions.

Some benefits of using questioning techniques as an effective communication skill include:

- To check your understanding of what is being said.

- To encourage the communicator to say more.

- In a meeting, for example, to facilitate participation.

- To help the communicator clarify his or her own understanding.

- To consolidate your own understanding of what is being said.

- To show enthusiasm or generate feelings for the conversation.

Therefore, in the context of questioning technique where open questions are non-directive and probe all feelings and emotions while building the dialogue, a closed question will be directive and lead to more specific information and detail being provided by the communicator.

Body language

This is a very complex area because while we can come up with some brief generalizations in this section, we are introducing ourselves to an area where there is much more learning to be done. Although we can say that paying attention to other people's body language can help us to understand others more effectively, behavioural scientists have much more research to do in this area. However, if as a listener we do pay attention to the body language of the communicator, we can get a reasonably clear feel for the communicator's genuineness, confidence and interest in what he or she is saying. Immediate areas to concentrate upon are the communicator's eye contact, expression, handshake and posture.

Some examples of more positive body language include:

- Good eye contact.

- Smiling.

- Relaxed posture.

- Perhaps leaning slightly forward.

Some examples of more negative body language include:

- Poor eye contact.

- Slouching.

- Crossed arms.

- Tense appearance.

- Body turned away from the other party.

Some general ideas are expressed above, although there are big dangers in being as general as this. For example:

a) We need to be aware of all consistencies or inconsistencies in what a person is saying and how body language complements the spoken word. Sometimes there will be consistency where a positive verbal message is met with a smiling face, an open stance. On other occasions there may well be a discrepancy between, for example, a person verbally agreeing to do something while looking solemn and having closed eyes. It then lies upon the listener to try to determine which aspect of the communicator's communication is the one to believe!

b) Not only are the general principles above ones to consider, they also mean different things depending on which part of the world we are referring to, or what type of culture is prevalent. We all need to be careful about invading an individual's *space*. Sometimes, in some cultures more than others (Western, for example) if an individual's *space* is encroached there will typically be an all-defensive response. Another general example would be eye contact which can be a very positive aspect of body language. Eye contact must not become a stare (implying an interrogation), although when eye contact becomes a stare it is a very different issue in, say, the United Kingdom compared to Japan and China.

Using your voice

How we use our voices gives the words we speak expression, emphasis, meaning and interest. The way we use our voices largely determines how we gain the attention of those to whom we are trying to communicate, and influences to a large degree how we can engage others in conversation.

While on the one hand we are learning something about being an effective listener, when we are communicating the tone of voice that we use should be appropriate and relative to what we are actually trying to say. Similarly when we are listening, we can look out for the correlation between the spoken word and the tone of voice.

Clearly, some ways in which tone can change the emphasis of what is being said can include connotations of being angry, happy, sad or persuasive. Quite often the tone of voice we use correlates quite naturally with the words we are saying. For example, if we are relaying something that is genuinely good news, our tone of voice will reflect that (*I am delighted to be here*). Alternatively, for example, in a sales scenario it is clear how a persuasive set of words and appropriate tone of voice can be complimentary (*I really do feel this is the best one on the market*). Equally, as I am sure you realize, depending on *how* these words are said, and, where that emphasis takes place, it can be very easy to recognize contradictions between the spoken word and the tone of voice.

Another option we have as communicators, and that a person communicating to us has, is to say nothing! In a *two-way* conversation, silence could mean or imply some of the following:

- That either party is uncomfortable.
- That one or both parties are being polite.
- That one party is buying time *to think*.
- Politeness.
- That one or even both parties do not know what to say next.

Being aware of how you come across

This area is clearly an important aspect of communicating, and some areas to think about include:

- What should to be done to always make a positive *first impression*.
- Personal grooming.
- How you dress.
- The particular messages you can give depending upon what style of dress you adopt.
- Personal posture.
- How you use consistent eye contact.
- The mannerisms (some very irritating!) that you use.
- How to appear more confident.

It is reasonable to say that how you are and how you appear to other people does send out clear messages. We all need to ensure that the messages we project are the ones that we want to project! There will be times when we want to be projecting different messages, depending upon, for example, where we are, whom we are seeing, why we are seeing them and what we are looking to achieve.

Effectively making a point

There are many different ways of discussing this area, although most of the popular models contain the same general principles and include the following four attributes of making your message effective:

Preparing your communication

In reality, we will not always have time to prepare properly prior to delivering a message. It is, however, important to prepare when it is right to do so, and also when we have the chance to do so. It makes good sense to think through what it is that we are trying to achieve when we are delivering a message, when it is the best time to deliver a message, and that you have got all your information correctly collated. In addition, and at the preparation stage, it is vitally important to consider who you are communicating with, what level of knowledge the other party will have, and how interested (or not!) they are likely to be about what you have to say. Ideally, prior to delivering any important message, we should be very clear in our own mind about what we are looking for the recipient of our message to do as a result. It may be possible to inform the recipient of this at the outset.

Gaining the attention of The receiver

A very important issue here is when and where you are going to make your communication. For example, last thing on a Friday afternoon may not be the best time to guarantee the attention of your time in a full team meeting!.

As a general rule, to gain somebody's attention, timing is critical, and it is usually best to go straight to the point that you are trying to make. It is never beneficial to apologise for your contribution at the outset, because this may well imply negative thoughts in the *receiver* which is something that should be avoided.

Making your message

On each occasion, when communicating to somebody else, you must speak clearly and in a focused way. Our research should have been done beforehand, and therefore any arguments we are using or information we are including should be relevant and correct.

Try always to be aware of how the other person may be feeling at the time you are making your point. Be responsive to body language and any comments or objections that are made.

If appropriate, invite questions from the recipient because this may well facilitate a two-way discussion, involve the other person in the discussion, and in any case will usually build the relationship.

It may well be a good idea to include regular summaries while making your message, as this not only gives regular opportunities to clarify your message, it also helps you as communicator to ensure that your message is being received as you would wish.

Checking understanding

Quite obviously, having delivered a message, we need to ensure that it has been appropriately received and understood.

Ways in which this can be done include:

- Being aware of the recipient's body language.

- By asking questions (either *open* or *closed* questions as we have seen earlier).

- If in doubt about whether a message has been received you may need to try again (and also review your own preparation on how effective this has been).

Written communication

Essentially, when you are writing, your primary objective is to gain the interest of your reader. What you write, the way in which you write it may or may not encourage your readers from reading anything that is in front of them.

What follows are some ideas that we all need to consider when writing. The list is not exhaustive, although the areas covered are usually accepted as being sensible, practical and heading towards *best practice*. The way in which we write is also influenced by our personal style, who we are intending should read what we have written, the culture of our organization, and what we are actually writing.

Using plain language

We all need to keep what we write as clear and as simple as possible – we all want our readers to understand what we are trying to say in the written word, and not to leave them trying to second-guess what we really mean.

Consider the following:

- Write in everyday language.

- Keep sentences simple and shorter rather than longer.

- Generally, use shorter words and words that are easier to understand.

- Be concise when possible.

- Try to make your writing sound natural, that is like the spoken word.

- Avoid jargon!

- If technical words or phrases are used for necessity, ensure that they are defined or explained.

Grammar

Attention to detail is important, and without doubt first impressions count. This will always be the case when somebody is reading an article – human nature being what it is – if there are misspellings, apostrophes missed out, no capital letters, for example, this is what the reader's thoughts will be diverted to, and not the content of the writing itself.

- *Abbreviations* – here it is very important to think of the reader. *Best practice* indicates firstly using capital letters for abbreviations and secondly giving the word or words in full for the first time (followed by the abbreviation that will be used in subsequent sections of your writing). Remember also that full stops in abbreviations are not always necessary.

- *Apostrophes* – when writing, a very common way to make a mistake! An apostrophe is used to *show possession*. An apostrophe can have either a singular or plural context, and is placed either side of the *s*, as the following example will illustrate: The *actor's* lines (only one actor); The *actors'* lines (more than one actor).

  Apostrophes can also be used to replace a missing letter (for example, *there's* no way forward as opposed to *there is* no way forward).

- *Capital letters* – capital letters are always used for the names of people, organizations, places and for political/geographical areas.

  Care needs to be taken when to use or not use capital letters and other than for the specific instances mentioned above, a general rule is to use lower case (i.e., not capital letters). Lower case would apply when writing a job title, the names of a committee or club, or for a geographical description.

- *Comma* – care should to be taken here because the primary purpose of a comma is to make meaning of a sentence more clear. Also, too many commas in any one sentence can cause confusion – it is likely that a sentence with too many commas is too long.

- *Paragraphs* – the basic concept here for the writer is similar to that when writing a sentence. Remember, for the reader a long paragraph can be like a long sentence, confusing! A balance has to be achieved, when writing, between using a paragraph to help *to break down* the text into sizeable portions for the reader. A paragraph can almost be seen as a pause between one area of the text and the next. It is also important not to make paragraphs too small either.

- *Bullet points* – these are used much more often in the written word these days because they enable writers to give various points they want to make more emphasis, and from the reader's perspective makes these points easier to see and digest. When writing, it is important that a consistent style of bullet point is adopted throughout and that a similar style for each series of bullet points used is also adopted.

There are, of course, other issues a writer needs to consider and these include the use of exclamation marks, dashes, hyphens, quotation marks, italics, and brackets.

Spelling and use of words

This is another important aspect of the written word. Getting spelling right and using the correct words is important, not only at the writing stage, but more importantly when considering the reader.

When writing, a consistent spelling style should be used and if in doubt the spelling of particular words should be checked thoroughly. Sometimes, when writing, one can almost become *blind* to any errors, and it is often helpful to get a colleague or a friend to have a thorough read through a piece of work prior to *going to print*.

When selecting which words to use, it is obviously important to use words that mean what you want them to mean. It therefore follows that words of ambiguity or words that are likely to cause confusion or misunderstanding should be avoided. This comes back to the principle we mentioned at the start of this section, about keeping sentences short, clear and simple.

Report writing

These days many of us are involved in writing reports, quite often for our line manager, sometimes to share with our colleagues, and on occasion to submit elsewhere in our business (for example, Head Office). Generally, a report should be as brief as realistically possible, clear and focused. Any report that you write will then have a better chance of being read, to provide information to the intended reader, to educate the reader accordingly, or even to provide some motivational benefits.

Planning a report

At this stage the writer of a report needs to be very clear about what it is the report is meant to be about. The report should have a topic or area to cover, and therefore the writer needs to consider what message or messages the report should be conveying to its readers.

Similarly, every report should have an objective – that is, to have some clarity about what the readers will learn, feel, or be expected to do as a result of having read the report.

Some examples include:

- A report containing detailed analysis, and well-structured and balanced arguments looking at the different perspectives of the analysis, and probably providing some clear conclusions and recommendations.

- A report that is intended to provide explanations to the readers. This type of report will be more factual, and possibly provide some element of instruction and guidance.

- Other reports may provide factual information and in this context will aim to give readers enough information, background and data to help to enable them to make a decision for themselves.

Obviously, at the planning stage of a report one main consideration is whom is the report targeted at. It needs to be clearly understood by the writer or author not only who will be receiving the report, but also their level of knowledge around the subject of the report, how you would generate the necessary enthusiasm and interest for the target audience to read your report, and who else may read the report at some point in the future.

Today, we are all *flooded* with paper from all directions– reams and reams of it. Each of us has more reading to do than we can either possibly cope with or realistically hope to digest. It is therefore clear that in writing any report, the writer has to earn the time of the reader not only to read the report, but to prioritize what you have written and for it to be seen as important enough to read in the first place.

The structure of a report

The structure of a report can be likened to the contents of a book; whatever structure a writer eventually adopts needs to be appropriate to the report that is being written.

Essentially, after the planning stage the writer may well have a mass of notes to coordinate into some kind of structure, and organizing all the information that is to hand is a good starting point. Then, depending on the subject matter of the report, a logical (and reader-friendly!) structure needs to be considered.

Quite often these days reports contain a series of headings throughout, which help to give the reader various *signposts* to assist him or her in finding their way around the report.

If headings are used in a report, they should be accompanied by a numbering system which will not only facilitate reference (with the use of an index), but also help the writer to structure the report into manageable parts. Once divided in sections, your report could also be divided even further, either by using sub-sections or bullet points.

Remember, that to use more than, say, three levels of division may cause confusion to the reader.

The contents of the report

The main parts of most formal reports are as follows:

- *The title page* – this contains the title of the report, details of author and usually the date of the report.

- A *contents page* – this enables the reader to have ease of reference throughout the report.

- *An executive summary* – the purpose of this summary is to provide an overview of the main points of the report itself and of the recommendations. Including an executive summary enables the reader to have an initial, quick and accurate overview of the report. It also means that if the report is going to be read at a later date, an overview can be obtained at the outset. Including a summary also means that the report can not only be read by your intended audience, but also by interested parties who may only require an overview of the contents.

- *The introduction to the report* – at this stage of the report, a clear indication of what is to follow is provided. An introduction should be clear, focused and concise. As we have mentioned before, the introduction should build a platform for what is to follow, and also provide clarity to the reader about the subject area and purpose of the report, and be written for the audience for which it is intended.

- *The main body of the report* – this is the main part of any report, and will contain the main sections or chapters of the report and include any facts/data, consider any evidence or background information, and look at any possible options for the ways ahead. Also at this stage, any costs, budget, and opportunity cost aspects must be considered – these days the financial dimension is of critical importance. Care needs to be taken at this stage as from the readers' perspective they will need to be clear as to what are the *main* points that are trying to be made, what are the *key* issues, and what really are the main features of the report. There is a clear danger that at the planning stage, with much information being assimilated for inclusion, the report may merely contain a mass of unstructured and mind-numbing information.

Some ways of overcoming this problem include: highlight each main message from the report and then support these messages by reasoned argument, background information and any relevant data; use graphics, charts or diagrams if appropriate to help illustrate facts and figures while also clarifying understanding; possibly summarize the main points that are covered in the report at regular intervals, again helping the reader to achieve clarity at regular stages.

- *Conclusions and recommendations* – firstly, the conclusions and recommendations should follow logically from what has been discussed in the main body of a report. The conclusions usually summarize the contents of the report, and provide some more general remarks about the main issues that have been covered. At the recommending stage, the writer is looking to project the ways forward, that is proposals for action (what happens next). These recommendations need to be clear, realistic and expressed in a way that will enable future progress to be measured. It is often helpful to include a detailed action plan at this stage which will show what needs to be done, who needs to be involved, what specific actions and responsibilities each person involved has, dates for progress to be reviewed, dates for particular activities.

- *Appendices* – the prime purpose here is to provide any additional information that may be required by some readers, although this particular aspect is not essential for *every* reader. Appendices may contain research material, additional background information, or particular parts of the report discussed in considerably more depth.

Writing the report

Some guiding principals at this stage, already mentioned earlier in this section, are as follows:

- Consider your audience.
- Be clear and concise.
- If necessary draft a first copy, re-read it and amend it and then *go to print.*
- Use clear language.
- Avoid jargon.
- Be careful with grammar.
- Use graphics when possible.
- Be careful with your presentation.

Communicating across a business unit

Effective communication is critical for the success of any business unit because the people within it need to be kept fully aware of all developments and in particular how these developments affect them personally. Communication should be two way, and team members should be aware that they work in an environment where their opinions can be expressed and are valued.

All of us need to communicate in many ways every day and some of us are more naturally skilled at communicating than others. We need to be clear, however, that communication is a skill – it is something that we can learn, and continue to develop throughout our career.

It is all too easy to glibly say that communication should be open, honest and regular. We not only need to understand what such words mean in terms of communication, we also need to understand how, in practical terms, they can *come to life* in the workplace:

- An open communication environment means that all issues that affect our teams and colleagues should be shared with them as soon as possible. In today's world of rapid change, there is plenty that needs to be communicated, and not all of this is necessarily good news. The credibility of any communication structure can only be enhanced by your being fully open with your team.

- A *golden* communication rule is that you should always be honest, clear and not open to misunderstanding or misinterpretation. Particularly in this working world of rapid change, communications need to be regular, sometimes even daily to be fully effective.

Planning the communication strategy

With the best will in the world, unless an ongoing activity of regular and focused communication is planned, the best intentions may not be fulfilled. A regular structure should be agreed between local management and team members to outline what meetings need to take place, for what purpose, with who is to attend and with what frequency. Once agreed, this structure should be made public, and possibly displayed on any staff notice board. Possible examples include:

- Management team meetings could be held weekly with all management to attend.
- Open forums could be held quarterly, with a cross-section of staff to attend.
- Section head meetings could be held fortnightly, with all section heads to attend.

Clearly, the structure for meetings at other communication events can be tailored to suit the particulars of the local business unit. As mentioned above, once this structure is agreed it should be made public to everybody within the business unit because this has the clear advantage of letting all other teams know when various communication events will be taking place and which ones they will play a key role in.

Team meetings

Meetings are a part of our daily life now and seem to be a very popular way of keeping colleagues fully briefed about what is happening in their organization and in their specific workplace. Every meeting involves in an investment of the attendees time and can involve significant cost (travel, accommodation, food, etc.) and opportunity cost (how much time in total used at the meeting could have been used productively elsewhere).

It is therefore imperative that meetings are seen to *add value* and they can do this if the following aspects are given close attention:

● For any formal meeting, ensure that agenda items are submitted beforehand. Agree with people who are submitting an item what areas they are looking to cover, what outcomes they are looking to achieve and how much time they will require at the meeting.

● All these details can be tabulated in the form of an agenda to be circulated. For example:

Agenda item	Sponsor (i.e., the person who has raised this issue for discussion)	Desired outcomes (i.e., what is expected to be achieved by raising this item at the meeting)	Time to be allocated to this issue
1.			
2.			
3.			
4.			
5.			

● Circulate details of the agenda beforehand to all parties.

● It may well be best to hold formal meetings more frequently as opposed to one much longer meeting less frequently.

● When a meeting is being held, ensure that all agreed action points are both recorded and have some commitment and structure. It must be specifically clear about who has ownership for progressing what particular area or action point that has been agreed.

● All areas of discussion/agenda items should be recorded, together with any agreed action points – these notes should then be circulated to all those in attendance.

● When possible, meetings should be held away from the regular work area; try to select a venue where the meeting will not be interrupted other than for a real emergency.

● Once arranged, cancel meetings only as the very last resort.

● It can be useful to *rotate the chair* at a meeting. This not only gives a developmental opportunity for some of the attendees, it also enables each meeting to be run in a slightly different way. Similarly responsibility for recording the events of the meeting (minute taking) should be shared around.

- If some of the meetings in a business unit are regular, then perhaps a standard agenda could be used.

Open forums/sessions

These occur where the unit manager/team leader/supervisor meets regularly with the team to discuss any subjects that are raised. If these are held regularly, then the principle of two-way communication can begin to become a reality.

Some guiding principles for holding an open forum include:

- Usually the most senior member of the management team holds these forums.

- To enhance the credibility of these forums, any issues raised, area of concern, and feedback requiring action should be dealt with as soon as possible. If necessary reconvene the group in order to give them the feedback they have requested.

- These open forums should be held at a frequency that is realistic for the size of the business unit. Probably this will be no less than quarterly.

- Ensure that there is a range of colleagues from across a business unit attending each open forum. This may mean a range of representatives across all sections within the business unit, and a range of grades to ensure that a realistic cross-section of opinion is obtained.

- Whoever is holding the open forum needs to ensure that everybody has the chance to contribute and make their point or give their opinion. Facilitation skills are very important here and are discussed elsewhere.

- Depending on the size of the business unit where the open forum is held, it may be that the attendees should introduce themselves to the rest of the group at the start of the meeting. Not only will this activity act as ice-breaker, it will also generate immediately some topics for discussion.

Newsletter

We have mentioned earlier in this section and are all individually aware of how much paper arrives on our desk each day. Some of this will always be read, some of it will go on a pending file, and some written communications will never be read. We must, therefore, find a way of making any newsletter that is available to colleagues and staff something that they would want to read. One way of doing this is to focus on *local* issues which are of interest and are also short and easy to read. It may be that an internal newsletter is produced by a team of staff from the business unit itself – this means the content can be decided from within the business unit and this in itself will generate interest.

Some ideas to include in a newsletter that will facilitate communication within a business unit will include:

- The manager's *column*.

- Staff issues – new recruits, staff leaving and any birthdays or weddings, for example.

- Sport and social activities.

- Recognizing success.

- Perhaps an article outlining the key areas covered at any open forum!

- Ongoing business issues.

- Any changes for the future.

- A competition or two!

- Any charity or social events.

Quite clearly, finding the resource to produce such newsletters is not easy for most of us. Nevertheless newsletters can be a good way of communicating with a team, and in this context they need to be produced reasonably regularly – on a quarterly basis.

The notice board

Using a notice can be an effective way of endorsing and supporting any communication, messages or issues that need to be conveyed. A staff notice can convey clarity, endorsement, and be a point of reference for further information as appropriate.

Notices need to be handled carefully and sometime sensitively, and as a general rule a notice should be displayed when it is used to convey a message that effects a whole business unit. In addition, all notices should be relevant and not out of date.

Responsibility

Everybody in a business unit has some responsibility for communicating, although ultimate responsibility for an effective approach to communication always rests with the unit manager.

We have already mentioned that today's working environment is one of rapid change and there are a multitude of issues that need to be managed on a daily basis – it may be an idea to appoint, if it is realistic to do so, one person who can coordinate all of the various issues involving communication.

This person could, for example:

- Act as editor for any in-house newsletter.

- Be responsible for the notice board, ensuring that all items displayed are both relevant and up-to-date.

- Organize the logistics for the ongoing agenda of communication events.

- Constantly review communication activities and try to think of ways of evolving the strategy, always looking for ways to improve.

3

Management of People

3.1   Leadership

Leadership is clearly a major factor in successful management. If a team is led well, then hopefully this team will respond by consistently good performance, and by being loyal and trustworthy. Some of the ways in which people can lead effectively include:

- *Lead by example* – an effective leader sets the example for all the effort and motivation that is required from the team itself. A leader's own efforts and levels of motivation show the team what you expect. Using the old maxim *behaviour breeds behaviour*, if the leader is not committed, then neither will the team be.

- *Setting clear goals* – the whole team, and each individual within the team, must clearly understand exactly what they are required to do and what standards of performance they are expected to achieve. In some cases, the objectives that need to be achieved are already determined, and in other cases the objectives (or standards or targets) can be achieved by consultation and discussion with the team members themselves.

- *Communication* – an effective leader is able to give the team all the information they need to do their jobs, and to keep them fully informed regarding any organizational issues both now and in the future. *Best practice* indicates the need to be as *open* as possible. As a general rule, if people are kept unaware or in the dark the *grapevine* will take over and in any case an environment of suspicion and lack of trust will soon develop. Communication, as we have seen elsewhere is a multi-dimensional process. Effective communication is two way in terms of being up and down, but it can also be lateral and diagonal communication as well. The implication here is that an effective leader needs to be both aware of what is happening, and to be able to listen and observe what is going on.

- *Delegating* – in the majority of cases, an effective leader should be able to delegate as much responsibility and authority as is realistically possible. An effective leader, then, achieves collective success through other people. *Leading by example*, does not mean that the leader does everything him or herself.

- *Recognize individuals' contributions* – this is where the value of each person's contribution to collective success is recognized. The ways in which each member of a team contributes to the overall objectives are inevitably different, and individual, and attention should be paid to individual needs and problems. Each member of the team needs to feel that his or her own contributions to the collective efforts are both recognized and appreciated.

- *Focusing on the importance of teamwork* – the emphasis on team-work is very important, involving a working environment in which team members work well with each other and interact well in work and probably socially as well.

- *Working well under pressure* – at these times, which are inevitable in reality, a leader should be seen to act in a calm or cool way. At a time of greater pressure, a leader must stay firm, focused and continue to make clear and appropriate decisions. Obviously, should the leader be seen to panic or act in an indecisive way, these actions will be highly visible to the members of team themselves, and there is a danger that whatever levels of respect existed, they will be lost.

- *Being fair and consistent* – there should be clear and visible standards for what is expected from everybody at their work, in terms of output and behaviour. The standards should be the same for everybody, with the primary aim of the team to be able to work in an environment of knowing what to expect, and knowing where they stand. The alternative, where a team does not know how their manager or leader will respond, or whether the the manager is in a good or bad mood, or where inconsistent decisions are being made, will clearly impact upon the working environment and ongoing rates of productivity.

There are many models or theoretical views on different leadership styles and we have considered some of these elsewhere. What follows is a simple exercise for you to gain some initial thoughts of where you would feature in your own leadership style and the continuum between being more directive (i.e., tell style) or more empowering (i.e., a more participative style).

Opposite are ten descriptions of ways of leading a team. For each one tick the box that is closest to your own attitude and management practice.

	I am a firm believer in this	I am fairly fairly keen on this	I am not really keen on this	I am strongly opposed to this
1. Closely managing people at all times.	☐	☐	☐	☐
2. Encouraging people to set their goals and standards themselves.	☐	☐	☐	☐
3. Allowing people to take on increasing responsibility.	☐	☐	☐	☐
4. Making sure people know that punishment for not performing is severe.	☐	☐	☐	☐
5. Continually pushing people to meet targets.	☐	☐	☐	☐
6. Spelling out all directions to people in complete detail.	☐	☐	☐	☐
7. Letting people plan their own work as much as possible.	☐	☐	☐	☐
8. Keeping worries about the company to myself.	☐	☐	☐	☐
9. Allowing people to make important decisions themselves.	☐	☐	☐	☐
10. Always seeking ways to extend people and broaden their contribution.	☐	☐	☐	☐

Transfer your answers to this list by circling your choice in each case.

	I am a firm believer in this	I am fairly keen on this	I am not really keen on this	I am strongly opposed to this
1	0	1	2	3
2	3	2	1	0
3	3	2	1	0
4	0	1	2	3
5	0	1	2	3
6	0	1	2	3
7	3	2	1	0
8	0	1	2	3
9	3	2	1	0
10	3	2	1	0

Total

Mark your score on the line below to show your preference within a range of possible management styles.

Tell style   Participating   style

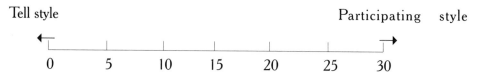

0   5   10   15   20   25   30

Clearly where you feature on this continuum will vary from time to time, and depend upon many factors – for example, the business unit in which you are working at the time, the team who you are working with, what work is being undertaken, the *local* culture, the timescales to complete that particular objective and what else is going on at the time. Nevertheless this exercise should have been thought-provoking to some extent and it may be useful for you to repeat it at regular intervals.

It is also a useful exercise to consider and observe various actions you take in carrying out some of the key aspects of leadership, or effective management. In addition, you can consider when and how your own line manager carries out some of these functions. Using specific examples is more meaningful simply because it focuses your mind on being specific rather than vague when looking for evidence. You could, for example, use the grid as opposite:

	Specific instances Your own	Examples Line management
Setting/agreeing objectives		
Planning		
Organizing		
Motivating		
Controlling		
Delegating		
Leading by example		

Managerial roles

So far in this section we have looked at some of the functions that an effective leader or manager needs to undertake on an ongoing basis. We can now move on and consider some of the roles that a manager or leader needs to take and again there are many views and opinions on this area – a consistent one is that a manager does not just have one role to play, but many roles, often undertaking many more than one at any given moment in time. Henry Mintzberg put forward a theory that argued that managers and team leaders spend their time either dealing with people, managing information, or making decisions. He categorized these areas into three:

- Interpersonal roles

- Informational roles

- Decisional roles

Within each of these three roles there are further sub-divisions, as follows:

- Interpersonal

- ◆ Figurehead
- ◆ Leader
- ◆ Liaison
- ● Informational
  - ◆ Monitor
  - ◆ Disseminator
  - ◆ Spokesperson
- ● Decisional
  - ◆ Entrepreneur
  - ◆ Disturbance handler
  - ◆ Negotiator
  - ◆ Resource allocater

As we have already seen, interpersonal roles are those that primarily involve managing people. Mintzberg argued that a manager needs to appear to others to be a manager and to act as a figurehead. Managers also need to be able to relate to and motivate their team, who will look to the manager as a leader. Also, a manager will need to deal with people outside of their own business unit, acting as a link between their unit and other parts of the organization – in other words being a point of liaison.

Mintzberg saw informational roles as those that focus on dealing with information inside and outside of the manager's particular business unit. This means that an effective manager should be aware of what needs to be known to make their own business unit or function to work well not only from an internal perspective but also as to what information from outside their own business unit would be useful to help to maximize business performance. Effectively the manager is acting as a *monitor* in this respect. This information needs to be communicated effectively throughout the business unit on an ongoing basis, and in this way the manager will be acting as (in Mintzberg's words) a *disseminator*. Finally, in this informational dimension a manager needs to relay information from his or her own business unit to other parts of the organization, or possibly even outside of the organization itself. In this context a manager is acting as a spokesperson.

Decisional roles are obviously concerned with the decisions that relate to the work being undertaken in a business unit. In this part of Mintzberg's model, he saw an entrepreneurial role whereby managers need to proactively seek opportunity to maximize the performance of themselves and their team against all competition (whether this competition is internal or external). The manager will have to handle problems that may arise unexpectedly, and may even have an impact (possibly drastic) effect on the ongoing operation of the business unit and will be acting as a *disturbance handler*. The ability to negotiate is also crucial, which means that the ability to reach ultimate agreement with others elsewhere in the business is essential while ensuring the overall business objectives are met. Finally, in this part of Mintzberg's model, he saw the ability to maximize the use of the available resources to manage as essential. These resources may be premises, budgetary, people, machinery, for example.

Management styles

A management style is effectively the way in which managers or team leaders manage and interact with their team and how they may involve their team in the decision making process. We can look at a continuum with at one extreme an autocratic style and the other extreme a participative style. We shall consider each of these styles in turn.

Autocratic style

This approach is one whereby the manager or team leader makes every decision without involving the team at all. This type of manager gives orders, using a *tell* style, and expects and probably demands obedience from the team. This type of style is often accompanied by implied threats or cohesion to ensure that the manager's orders are carried out. Managers who adopt this particular style do not expect or require any creativity or input from their team members.

Benevolent autocratic

A manager adopting this type of style will, in a similar way to the autocratic style of manager, make every decision without involving the team. One difference is that in adopting this particular style this type of manager has some consideration for the team members. Although benevolent autocratic managers demand obedience from their team, threats are not necessarily used as the only way to achieve results. This type of manager requires team members to carry out their instructions for their own benefit, with some form of reward or recognition when they do so (or possibly some kind of threat or disincentive if they do not). However, in a similar way to the autocratic manager, the benevolent autocratic does not expect nor ask for any input or ideas from team members.

Consultative style

The consultative manager consults the team before making decisions and requests ideas and suggestions, and approaches every issue that arises in a joint way. In this context, the manager always takes full responsibility for any decisions made, and the decision when it is made is that of the manager. In other words the manager has the final say.

Participative style

This type of manager shares all and every decision with the team. On every occasion the team gets together and collectively agrees the way ahead. The manager then has responsibility for implementing the decision made, and his or her own experience and expertise will have played only a contributory part in reaching this decision. The manager's role is one of actually authorizing and ensuring that the decisions once made are carried out.

All managers tend to have one dominance, which is the style that they use instinctively. In reality, also, at different times or in different circumstances any manager could display more than one of the above styles.

A summary of the main advantages and disadvantages of each of the four styles can be seen below:

Autocratic
Main advantage
- Can achieve results quickly (particularly in the short term).

Main disadvantage
- Will not motivate team members.

Benevolent autocratic

Main advantage
- Can incentivize team members through reward and recognition.

Main disadvantage
- Does not take advantage of initiative or ideas from the team.

Consultative

Main advantage
- Incorporates and welcomes ideas from the team.

Main disadvantage
- No concept of empowerment or decision making authority given to the team.

Participative

Main advantage
- Lets everybody feel involved in the decision making process.

Main disadvantage
- Because of everybody's involvement this style can be slow and cumbersome.

3.2   Coaching

Within our working world, it is inevitable that change is always taking place, and at an increasing rate. There are always going to be new initiatives, and organizational change, new objectives, higher targets or increased business to obtain. Coaching is one way that can help to develop a team to deal with the rapid world of change, albeit as only one factor among many others.

When initiating a coaching exercise, there are many factors to consider. Some of these are given below.

Making the decision to coach

● As coach you need to consider where coaching is appropriate and will *add value* to your business unit.

● From the outset, any coaching initiative needs to be expressed in terms of specific (business) results and the coach and *coachee* need to be very clear about what they are trying to achieve.

● Whoever is to be the coach, he or she must be respected members of the team, have well developed interpersonal skills, and have the capacity to take on increased responsibility.

Consider which style of coaching to adopt

There are many different styles of coaching, for example:

● For a coach to observe an individual's particular strengths and weaknesses and give guidance and feedback.

● Use a *role play* scenario to either illustrate a particular set of circumstances, or to practise these skills.

Identify the *coachee*

● Clearly, coaching is an investment, and anyone who needs to be coached must be somebody who will benefit from this investment.

● In this context, coaching needs to be focused on an area of the business unit that will clearly be improved as a result.

Monitoring the results of coaching

● Clearly this is critical, because only by monitoring what is being done will the coach and *coachee* be able to see and identify the progress that is being made.

● Throughout, while monitoring progress, regular reviews must take place to ensure that progress is being analysed and both coach and *coachee* are comfortable that things are going to plan. Undoubtedly, the environment for successful coaching is largely driven by the coach's skill and enthusiasm, together with managerial support.

We need to be very clear that the managers themselves do not have to be the actual coaches, although sometimes this will be the case. This means the managers either do the coaching, or are very visible in the support they provide to the coaches themselves. Coaching needs to be given a priority on the business unit, because this in itself will give the coach the necessary authority to carry out their responsibilities.

Throughout, the coach must project a personal interest in the *coachee's* endeavours. Throughout the coach must be giving constructive and non-judgmental feedback to the coachee because regular guidance and counselling is essential. The whole exercise can be a great motivator for both coach and *coachee* because it should be focusing on the personal development of both parties.

Coaching and training

Elsewhere, we shall be considering the training process as a whole and shall see that part of this process includes preparing an individual for the training event (pre-training event briefing) and subsequently de-briefing a training event with the participant involved. What is essential is that the benefits of a training course are translated to the workplace as soon as possible. One way of facilitating this process is coaching and thinking very clearly about the costs of not coaching and allowing an individual to go back to old habits after the training event.

With coaching, the impact of a training event can be sustained in the workplace. Clearly, however, an investment in coaching can never *guarantee* a return because individual development can be unpredictable. Nevertheless a coach is in a very good position to monitor the return an individual can give to a business unit after the training event, by using coaching as a proactive method of support.

Some thoughts to consider in this respect are as follows:

- Coaching can help to consolidate knowledge required on a training course.

- Coaching can enable training to be translated into *the real world*.

- Coaching, in this context, can help to reinforce the value of training to other people in the business unit.

- Individuals can easily forget the skills they learn on a training course, so follow-up coaching can be invaluable as a reinforcement exercise.

- Coaching does not involve inventing work – it is an exercise that is done in the workplace, and therefore focuses on work/tasks that need to be done in any case.

Coaching and appraisal

Best practice indicates that a team leader/business unit manager/manager should ensure that each of his or her team has regular performance reviews, probably at least minimally on a formal quarterly basis, and culminating in an annual appraisal review. Inevitably, throughout the appraisal year an individual will have shown evidence in job performance of success and areas requiring development. Coaching is an excellent way of working with an individual to improve development areas, although both the appraiser and appraisee in the first instance, and the coach and the *coachee* (appraisee) need to be sure that the right areas are being focused on to gain maximum benefit from any coaching investment. In this context, we need to be aware that:

● Coaching when linked to an individual's development needs, as highlighted by an appraisal, can accelerate that individual's development. Appraisers can play a key role in identifying these development needs and arranging for the support of a coach to be available.

● For these developmental needs to be identified, a working environment of openness, honesty and trust clearly needs to exist.

● By working with an individual to focus on their development needs, there should be not only increased job performance, but hopefully also increased job satisfaction for the individual concerned.

● This means that the coaching must be directed to an individual's goal in a specific way. Quite possibly, then, in this context coaching can be quite directive and deal with a specific developmental/problem area.

● Invariable the coaching will be very visible, and therefore may need to be managed quite sensitively, and it may also motivate others to ask for this kind of support.

Providing the necessary support

The relationship between the manager/coach and the *coachee* is a critical one; it needs to be based on trust, a two-way relationship, and be well structured and focused.

● By supporting the *coachee* it will help to improve their job performance.

● As the coaching progresses it may be that additional areas for development are discovered.

● Throughout, when the coach is providing support, he or she must be positive with guidance and feedback, and avoid at all costs being judgmental and damming. This will help to create an environment of trust and respect and give the *coachee* the maximum opportunity to benefit from the coach's support.

● The coach needs to be approachable, aware of the challenges and difficulties the *coachee* may face, and receptive to any requests for help.

● *Best practice* indicates that coaching needs to be a regular and planned event, so that both coach and *coachee* can prepare properly. In all probability, coaching done on a random and ad hoc basis will not work as well.

● There is no doubt that the support of a coach is critical and requires a considerable time commitment. We need to be very clear that this time commitment does not have an aim to enable the *coachee* to become totally dependent upon the coach; it is about enabling the coachee to become more independent.

The coaching process

Identify the coachee

The likely coachee is going to be a member of a team:

● For whom coaching will have an immediate impact on job performance.

● Who does best at work, and who recognizes the benefits of self development.

● Who if possible, is a member of a team who will not only benefit individually from any coaching support, but will also enable others in the team to see what is possible from being supported in this way.

Setting up the relationship between a coach and coachee

This is a very important stage because there are some very significant areas to be considered at the outset. These include the following:

● Organizing regular meetings between the coach and *coachee*. Ensure these commitments are logged in diaries and actually happen.

● A relationship of trust and confidentiality needs to be established from the outset between the coach and *coachee*.

● Although the business unit will be looking to see a return on the investment in coaching, any coaching activity will work to its optimum when it is not formally assessed.

● It is quite possible that the coaching itself will imply that the *coachee* is being tried out for the first time or developing new skills in a *live* workplace situation. The coach needs to be aware that the *coachee* may be feeling a level of discomfort at this stage.

● It needs to be very clearly established that coaching is a positive activity. The two-way relationship of trust and confidentiality means that issues can be discussed openly and without fear of recrimination. In no way is coaching intended to be critical.

● The coach needs to ensure that the *coachee* will be fully committed to this exercise, as there will be times when results from any coaching will not be immediate.

● Throughout the coaching process, progress will be enhanced if the *coachee* is able to both be open to new ideas on how to work, and additionally contribute his or her own ideas and thoughts of how progress may be made.

Establishing what to focus the coaching activities on

At this stage, there needs to be an early understanding of what the coachee's actual needs are. Any coaching activity should be focused on the coachee's own agenda so that he or she has ownership of the activities being committed to. At one of the early meetings between coach and *coachee*, the coach should be discussing the *coachee's* own ideas for development and clearly key attributes of the coach at this stage are to be listening well to what the *coachee* is saying and questioning appropriately to establish, understand and clarify the *coachee's* needs.

It may be that it takes a little time to understand the *coachee's* developmental needs. They may not have been obvious from, say, an appraisal interview or recent job performance, although some possibilities are as follows:

a) Lack of knowledge – it may be straightforward because the *coachee* does not know what to do, or perhaps is not clear what the job actually entails.

b) The *coachee* may not have the necessary skills to undertake duties to the required standard. In other words the *coachee* knows what to do but is not quite clear how to do it.

c) The *coachee* may have an attitudinal problem, possibly due to lack of motivation, seeing part of the job as unrealistic or unachievable, or feeling lack of recognition for doing this activity.

d) It is possible that the coach forms an early opinion that the *coachee* is in the wrong role – this clearly creates a different set of issues, as it is unlikely that coaching will be the solution here!

Creating a plan to coach

At this stage the coach is considering how to help to plan, prepare and make a constructive effort to facilitate the *coachee's* learning.

It is likely that the coach needs to consider:

- That the whole process needs to be planned.

- That the coaching process may well need to be adapted over time, either as circumstances change or new development needs for the coaching are identified.

- Ensure progress is regularly reviewed, and achievable and realistic targets are discussed and agreed by the coach and the *coachee* at the outset.

- It is usually more realistic to work for a longer-term and sustainable improvement in the job performance of the *coachee*, rather than looking for *a quick fix*.

- During this planning stage it is very important that *coachees* are aware of when they will have the opportunity to develop new skills, how they will acquire these new skills, and what they can expect to do differently as a result.

- It therefore follows that an effective coach will be fully involved in the planning of the coaching itself, and be there to support the learning process.

Reviewing the coachee's progress

As we mentioned earlier, it is essential that regular reviews are made and at each meeting between the coach and the coachee both positive and negative aspects of progress should to be covered.

As a general rule, these review meetings should always end on a positive note and throughout feedback provided to the *coachee* should be as specific as possible (i.e., based on actual events and using specific data relating to these). Furthermore, throughout the coaching process, there are some prevalent things that need to be adhered to:

a) When providing feedback and guidance to the *coachee*, the coach must achieve a realistic balance between positive and negative guidance. Clearly, positive feedback will cover what has gone well. Negative feedback will focus on areas that are still not proceeding as planned and therefore may need to be sensitively shared with the coachee.

b) With all the feedback that is provided by the coach, maximum benefit will be obtained if the *coachee* obtains absolute ownership of this feedback. This means that the coachee fully understands why the feedback has been given and is fully aware of what needs to be done to either continue developing positive attributes or to carry on working at improving developmental aspects of job performance. In this context, the coach will have input, although in no way should the coach be seen as a judge – an integral part of the review process is to accommodate the coachee's view of what happened so that there is a two-way discussion and ultimate agreement upon not only what happened in the past, but what should be happening in the future.

c) By providing specific feedback to the *coachee*, the coach is helping the learner to self-assess the results of actions. Here the coach will discuss, in detail, specific instances of the coachee's behaviour and probably comparing what actually happened with what was meant to happen. By undertaking an open and honest discussion of the reasons for the specific behaviour of the coachee, the coachee will gain a fuller awareness of what needs to happen differently in the future.

Behaviours of the coach and coachee

So far we have looked at various aspects of the coach/coachee relationship, of what should be happening throughout the process, and underpinning these various dimensions will be the behaviours of both parties.

We have already seen that this relationship should be two-way, open, honest and ongoing. In addition:

i) Behaviours focused on the coach will include the coach giving opinions: his or her own ideas and feedback to the *coachee*. They will also involve the coach sharing his or her knowledge or expertise to the coaching.

ii) Behaviours focused on the *coachee* will make him or her feel much more involved in the process and have ownership of any agreed outcomes. An ideal coaching scenario is one where the coachee is encouraged to and feels comfortable in talking about his or her own ideas and solutions to any issues that arise during the whole process.

Obviously the exact balance between coach- and *coachee*-focused behaviours will depend on the particulars of each coaching relationship. What is essential is that the balance between the two parties is exactly right for each occasion.

Some other behaviours of an effective coach to be aware of include:

- When observing the *coachee* in action, observe very carefully although not in an intimidating way – you will then be able to record specifically action is being undertaken in order to provide accurate feedback.

- Throughout the process always ask questions to check your own understanding of what is being achieved. This will help to clarify both the coach's and *coachee's* understanding of what has been achieved so far.

- Build up empathy with the *coachee*.

- Avoid lecturing to the *coachee*.

- Always endeavour to encourage a two-way dialogue between the coach and *coachee*.

- Throughout try to build the confidence of the *coachee*.

- Remember that the *coachee* is not being *formally* assessed; it is therefore very important that the coaching relationship is kept as informal as possible.

- Although the ownership of the benefits of the coaching process will rest with the *coachee* and the coachee should feel empowered to be responsible for his or her own development, the coach needs to achieve the right balance between being directive and non-directive when clarifying the expectations of the whole process.

- Always show understanding and awareness of what the *coachee* is going through.

- Be fully aware that coaching involves a considerable investment in your time, as without this commitment the ultimate benefits will not be achieved.

3.3   Mentoring

Some of the main rules of a mentor to an individual are to give moral support to a colleague, be there to listen, provide an unthreatening presence, and to give sensible advice, or just to be there to chat something through.

Mentoring is an important role and ideally a mentor should be carefully selected and trained for that task. This is because a mentoring relationship is one whereby the mentor helps other people within the organization to learn more about themselves, and their own potential and capability. In fact this relationship can be informal or formal it need make no difference to the effectiveness of this relationship.

Many organizations are introducing mentor systems to help to support their staff development programmes. This seems to be a strategy that works, is cost effective and provides potential personal satisfaction for those who become involved in it (i.e., become mentors).

There seems to be three generic characteristics of the mentoring process:

● Mentoring is a one-to-one activity.

● Mentoring sees personal, professional and skill development as a priority.

● Mentoring is a particular type of support process within the training and development process.

There are various approaches to being a mentor, and here are some examples:

a) A mentor can be a trainer, and in this sense will be the *expert*. The mentor here will have the role of organizing the training, teaching as appropriate, being the source of knowledge and probably providing some form of instruction.

b) The mentor can take the role of a friend and confidant. In this case the mentor may be no more expert in a particular area than the person being mentored. Here the mentor takes the role of providing support, possibly in a relationship between two people of equal status. With this emphasis, both partners in the mentoring relationship have equally as much to gain from their involvement. Examples of this type of mentoring are guiding, counselling, facilitating or discussing a particular issue.

c) A combination of the first two options above. This means a mentor may be fulfilling a dual role, say providing some training while concurrently being there as a friend or to provide support.

Characteristics of a successful mentor

A mentor is a skilled person, and needs to exhibit at least some of the following characteristics:

● Being flexible.

● Becoming actively involved in the mentoring role and showing an interest in the person being mentored.

● Looking at alternative ways of making progress in a reliable and quick manner.

● Showing respect to the learner.

● As necessary, being patient while always being friendly.

● Being willing and able to spend time with the learner, essentially as long as it takes.

● Being aware of and sensitive to the learner's problems and trying to see things from the learner's point of view.

● Quickly generating a feeling of trust with the learner and generating enthusiasm for the whole experience.

This essentially means that not everybody is suitable to be a mentor!

In addition a good mentor, while dealing with the learner on a personal level, must have the credibility and knowledge in the first place. This may mean that a mentor must review his or her own skills and knowledge and fill in any gaps. An effective mentor will also have thought over any potential problems or challenges before they happen, and have begun to consider what they will need to do when these problems arise. Of course, mentors have to be able to help their learners by presenting what they know in the best possible way and thereby helping the learner to make the maximum progress that is realistically possible. Ideally, a mentor will have a good understanding about how people learn and what facilitates this process and what can hinder it.

The advantages of mentoring

Advantages for the organization

These include:

- To influence positively staff retention levels and improving an organization's reputation in the recruitment marketplace.
- Contributing towards a more effective communication process throughout the organization.
- A very cost-effective way of providing individual development.
- A factor in improving the overall development of people within an organization.

Advantages for the mentor

These include:

- Probably increased job satisfaction.
- An opportunity to learn.
- A sense of fulfillment in helping other people.

Advantages for the learner

These include:

- Tangible evidence of how the organization is prepared to help with learning and development.
- Having regular contact with somebody else within the organization who is there to give and share knowledge and experience.
- A chance to develop and learn in a non-threatening way.

Potential disadvantages of the mentoring process

- We all live in the real world, and although we should look for the positive elements of such a process there are some potential pitfalls we need to be aware of.
- Clearly, there will be resource implications for both the mentor and learner. Time needs

to be invested in this process, and both the learner and mentor may need to undergo some type of training so that they can gain full benefit from the process.

- Although mentoring can add value in its own way, it should in no way be seen as a replacement for ongoing training and development.

- An organization needs to ensure that only the right people are selected to be mentors. A wrongly selected mentor can be dangerous!

3.4   Making a presentation

In today's world, part of the essential attributes of a supervisor/team leader/manager are to be able to talk effectively in front of a group of people. That is, making a presentation – a presentation is one of the many ways in which a team leader can communicate with colleagues, or relay information to a group of people from outside the organization.

In the pages that follow we shall consider what needs to happen to make a skilful and effective presentation.

Planning a presentation

The key considerations when planning a presentation are:

- Setting your objectives.
- Establishing who your audience will be.
- Considering how you will actually make your presentation.
- Considering the contents of the presentation.

As with most things, planning is essential, as without an effective plan a presentation will not have a robust structure and the content may well be unclear.

Once objectives have been set for your presentation they will be very useful for:

- Planning the presentation.
- Eliminating irrelevant material.
- Ensuring that the required learning occurs.
- Enabling the audience to focus attention on known and clear objectives. Once the objectives for a presentation have been decided, an immediate logical structure is ready made. Nevertheless, objectives for a presentation must be:

  ♦ Clear (stated in clear, simple language so there is no doubt about what an objective is saying).

  ♦ Brief (to provide clarity rather than confusion).

  ♦ Practical and understandable (also realistic, in order that they can be achieved during the presentation itself – do not be too ambitious).

- ◆ Stated in terms that the audience will understand (in terms of how the audience will behave after a presentation).

Clearly, the way in which a presentation is prepared will vary depending on who your audience is. It is essential that a presenter is fully aware of who is going to be attending as well as:

- The size of the audience. Think about the differences of presenting to a group of 6 to 10 people and to a group of 20.

- Their current knowledge levels. Clearly, a presenter should avoid giving a presentation on a subject in which the audience is already fully qualified – inevitably the audience would sleep well in this event!

- If possible, do some research beforehand to try to gauge your audience's current knowledge levels.

By gaining an understanding of your audience it can then be considered how you will approach the presentation itself. Some presentations can be, quite rightly, formal, others informal, partly driven by the subject to be discussed, the venue, the audience's background, and the impact required, and the time available.

Remember also that when the contents of the presentation are considered the eventual presentation should contain all the ingredients that your audience would want to hear. As mentioned above, one general objective for all presentations is to ensure your audience learns something, not sleeps well throughout!

The structure of a presentation

Following on from the section above, a presentation is to be presented in a clear and logical format. Two of the main benefits here are that it will help the presenter present and help the audience to understand.

Usually a presentation consists of three main and general parts:

i) The opening.

ii) The main body of the presentation.

iii) The close/conclusion.

In some ways the structure of a presentation can be likened to the chapters in a book or an agenda at a meeting – the connections being that the audience need to be clear about what is happening throughout, about what will happen throughout, what will then happen at each stage, probably having regular reviews, and pulling it all together (concluding) and pointing to the ways ahead.

We shall now consider each aspect of the structure of a presentation.

The opening

At this stage of the presentation there are many things to consider, all of which are important in their own way, each of which must be given adequate attention at the start of the presentation. These are:

- Be clear about the purpose of the presentation.

- Outline the main areas to be covered during the presentation.

- Indicate how long the presentation will take (then manage this time effectively!).

- Will handouts/presentation material be available or will the audience need to take notes?

- How you are going to attract the attention of an audience at the beginning of a presentation.

- Keep any opening part of the presentation short and focused.

- Consider, and give clear guidance at the start of a presentation, how questions will be dealt with. The two main options here are to take questions at any time throughout the presentation, or to request that all questions are kept until the end.

The main body of the presentation

This part of your presentation is the main part of what an audience will hear. It will be the main strength of any presentation and for immediate consideration is how a presenter will make the body of a presentation easy for the audience to understand. This usually means that a presentation is divided into sub-sections (similar to chapters in a book), each of which can act as *headings* for different parts of the presentation and also as *signposts* to give a clear indication both to the presenter and the audience as to what stage of the presentation they are at. Sometimes, partly depending on the length of the presentation and the complexity of the topics covered, it is helpful to the audience (and to the presenter!) to briefly review each part of the main body of the presentation prior to proceeding to the next part.

The close/conclusion

This stage of the presentation is near to the end and a presenter will be looking to summarize what has gone before, ask the audience if they have any questions (and the questions have been taken throughout the presentation) and to then thank your audience for their time, and if appropriate their contributions.

In the concluding remarks or summary the audience should hear nothing new. The aim here is merely to briefly review what has gone before. Earlier on we mentioned that there were two basic options of how to handle questions. If the presenter decided to take questions throughout, then the end of the presentation will be the final opportunity for an audience to put any questions they may have. Alternatively, the presenter may well have asked the audience to keep all questions to this time in the presentation, and therefore any questions must be dealt with here. In some ways, an audience will be very watchful of how a presenter handles questions as a measure of his or her credibility. One golden rule is to answer the questions directly, honestly and as concisely as you can. It is usually advisable to avoid question time becoming a *one-to-one* debate with a single member of the audience. Another golden rule is that should a member of the audience ask a question to which the presenter does not know the answer, the presenter must say so! Inevitably, if presenters decide to *make it up as they go along* a member of the audience will already have *called their bluff*. An effective presenter will admit openly that they do not know the answer, but will endeavour to find out and let the questioner know in due course. The end of the presentation is the final opportunity for the presenter to reinforce the key elements of the messages that have been contained throughout the presentation. Effectively it is like a climax to a mystery, the conclusion to a fireworks display, an opportunity to deliver a final powerful reinforcement of the main element of the presentation itself.

Selecting your visual aids

A visual aid is a valuable part of any presentation, because it can reinforce the messages to be given throughout the presentation. A visual aid can prompt and reinforce in the audience's mind the ideas and concepts that are to be covered throughout the presentation. Many presenters prefer to use pictures because they can be more vivid, convey messages that may be difficult to verbalize, save time, stimulate interest and add variety to a presentation.

The most popular form of visual aid is an overhead projector, which can be an extremely useful visual aid and will enable the presenter to face the audience throughout. With an overhead projector the overhead slides themselves can vary in complexity, or in fact increase in complexity by using a series of transparent overlays. The presenter can also write on the transparencies during the presentation or point out details quite easily on the slides themselves.

Some golden rules for using an overhead projector include:

- Ensure the slides to be used for the presentation are prepared and in sequence to run alongside the contents of the presentation itself.

- Keep the overhead projector switched on only when you want the audience to see the slide. Once this has been done and for all other periods during the presentation, switch the overhead projector off.

- When presenting, the presenter should never stand in front of the overhead projector, risking the danger of the audience having an obscured view.

- If the presenter uses slides with a frame, the presenter can write his or her own prompt notes on these which can often be quite helpful.

- All slides should be simple, bold, and if possible contain pictures rather than words.

Some presenters use a flip chart to facilitate their presentation. Flip charts are simply large paper pads on which the visuals to be used have been prepared beforehand. One advantage of using a flip chart is that it can be prepared before the presentation itself, and will undoubtedly be more effective than a flip chart illustration constructed during the presentation itself unless you happen to be Rolf Harris! One key danger here is that flip charts are not usually suitable for very large audiences, and the presenter should ensure that anything drawn on flip charts is visible to the whole of the audience.

If the presenter uses slides, which can be appropriate for a large audience, the presenter has additional flexibility. This is because sequences can be altered, interrupted, and timings varied. Obviously, the presenter needs to be very familiar with the equipment being used, and therefore practice is essential – the credibility of the presenter will be reduced if the slide projector *sticks* or shows slides upside-down. In addition, when slides are being shown the room will be darkened which means that for this period of time the presenter will lose eye contact with the audience.

Films can also be a most absorbing supplement to a presentation, although they must be used with some caution. A film should be used, as should any other visual aid, to supplement a presentation not to provide an interlude or entertainment.

Dealing with interruptions and objections from the audience

Anybody making a presentation not only must have a robust plan, a clear structure and objectives and have prepared and rehearsed thoroughly, they must also be prepared to be interrupted (legitimately or otherwise) or to have a member of the audience raising a disagreement or objection.

During a presentation these types of interruptions can be made for many reasons, and it is more often the case that the interruption will be made because a member of the audience wants to clarify a particular point. Sometimes, however, a *fast ball* will be thrown by a member of the audience to try and catch out the presenter or even to lay a trap or interrupt the flow of a presentation.

As a presenter you can stay in control of your presentation if you are interrupted by:

- Having any issues raised during the presentation on a flip chart and dealing with each of these at the end of your presentation.

- Never take any interruption personally.

- Try not to look flustered.

- Listen very carefully and attentively to any issue that is raised and show an interest in the point that is being made.

- If necessary, check your understanding of the issue that has been raised by *reflecting back* using your own words.

- If, as the presenter, a mistake has been made, be honest and admit this – all presenters are human!

- Once an issue has been dealt with, ensure that the question/objection has been handled to everybody's satisfaction.

- Of the many reasons why an individual may interrupt a presentation some are:

  ◆ An individual does not agree with what is being said (probably depends on how controversial the subject matter is).

  ◆ A member of the audience is seeking to impress somebody (probably his or her boss!).

  ◆ Somebody likes to show that he or she is smarter or more knowledgeable than the presenter.

  ◆ Somebody just does not like being in a presentation.

  ◆ For, probably an irrational reason, somebody does not like the presenter on a personal level.

Either way, a presenter will become more competent at dealing with interruptions or objections as he or she becomes more experienced in delivering effective presentations. As mentioned above the golden rule is never to take any interruption personally.

Brief conclusion

What we have said on the preceding pages outlines the techniques and skills we use to learn and accommodate prior to making a presentation. Undoubtedly, all this hard work will go to waste unless a presenter spends a considerable amount of time practising beforehand. This practice will not only enable a presenter to become familiar with the material, it will also become clearer how long the presentation will take and also give the presenter a chance of actually testing the proposed presentation prior to *going live*.

There is an old saying "To fail to prepare means that you prepare to fail"!

3.5   Facilitation skills

Facilitating is the ability to help others to express their views. This ability is very important when maybe leading a group discussion involving either your colleagues or customers, as part of a presentation (when trying to find out the views of your audience), perhaps at a meeting, or during a one-to-one event (for example, an appraisal or coaching discussion).

The ability to facilitate means you need to avoid the temptation of letting your own views dominate. For example, if you are facilitating a group discussion, then by far most of the imput needs to come from the group itself, and not from the facilitator! Also, when facilitating and creating the environment for others to express their views, it may be that you hear views that are different to your own. A good facilitator avoids feeling defensive or threatened if this should arise.

We shall now consider some important aspects of facilitating.

Involving others

This means that *open* questions are often used because it is this type of question that invites others to respond with more than a *yes* or *no* answer. These type of questions usually begin with *how, what, why, where, when,* for example. For purposes of clarity, it is sometimes useful to request a specific example from other people because this will enable some actual data to become available as well as feelings. Similarly, a facilitator must be aware of the feelings behind the facts.

Confirming your understanding

When you are inviting the opinions of others, then quite clearly it means you have to listen to them! This actually means listening to what the other person is saying and not just keeping quiet while being totally preoccupied with other thoughts at the same time! The appropriate body language can be an indication that you are listening to somebody else. For example, good eye contact (not a stare!) or nodding occasionally are good indications. Also, as appropriate, it can be useful for a facilitator to check that he or she has understood what has just been said by asking questions to clarify.

Encouraging others to respond

When you are inviting others to give their opinions, you will probably get a variety of responses; some people will feel very comfortable in giving their views others will feel quite uncomfortable. An effective facilitator needs to recognize and value comments that are made even if this means just saying *thank you* or *I think that is a very useful idea.* Similarly, if an individual comes forward with a view that is either personal or destructive, a facilitator can effectively challenge this member of the group/audience to do some re-thinking. In this set of circumstances, there is a clear need to avoid coming across as being threatening.

Directing a discussion

This means that when a meeting, whether one-to-one or with a group, is to be facilitated, there needs to be some clear end goal or objective. These objectives need to be clarified beforehand so that you as facilitator and the other people involved know what it is that they are aiming for. This may mean that there is an agenda to work to, so that both the facilitator and everybody else have some common ground to work towards. It will inevitably mean that the facilitator summarizes activity regularly so that all parties know exactly where they are.

Handling disagreements or conflicts

One potential danger in inviting the opinions of others through effective facilitation is that in this open and honest environment there may be a need to build common ground to avoid disagreements. In these circumstances, a facilitator must avoid a situation where people focus so much on their disagreements that the discussion grinds to a halt. By having an end objective or clear purpose for a meeting or gathering, it should be possible for the facilitator to refocus attention on what everybody should be aiming for. If necessary, time could be spent focusing on the areas of disagreement prior to moving on.

4

SELECTION, RECRUITMENT AND THE INDUCTION PROCESS

4.1 Selection and recruitment

Why is recruitment important?

It is very likely that the early stages of a recruitment process are the first time that a potential employee practically interacts with an organization. Therefore whatever happens as a result of the recruitment process itself (i.e., whether eventual employment is offered or not) it is very important that the process itself is both professional and leaves those involved with a positive impression of the organization. Word spreads very quickly in the marketplace, among customers or clients, about poor practices in the areas of recruitment and selection. Furthermore, second-rate practices in these areas for those who are actually employed mean that the early days of employment are most likely filled with negative impressions of the organization, which may well mean people are looking for their second job before they have completed their induction on the first one!

Some elements of best practice

- An organization's recruitment inspection policy should be visible and communicated to all employees.

- Equal opportunity policies should be publicly endorsed in both theory and practice.

- The recruitment and selection procedures themselves must be seen to be fair in approach, consistent in application, and relevant to the current employment market.

- Job advertisements, whether internal or external, must be accurate and realistic.

- It is very preferable for all those members of staff that are involved in the recruitment and selection process to be adequately trained and experienced in these roles.

- Job advertertisements must not contain any elements of *ageism*.

- To maintain the positive impressions given of the organization at all times, all applications for employment (at the recruitment stage) or selection should be acknowledged.

The main elements of a recruitment procedure

Job specification

This is the first stage, and a job specification aims to identify the requirements and purpose of a job. A job specification should be made up of the following features:

a) The knowledge, skills and aptitudes required to do the job.

b) The type of relevant experience required to do the job.

c) What competencies are required to do the job.

d) What training is available to help candidates in their new role, as required.

e) Any personal qualities or circumstances, although these must be directly relevant to the job and not contradicting any aspects of equal opportunities for ageism, for example.

The application form

An application form must be appropriate to the job that is being advertised. This means any information requested should be relevant to the job itself or to the selection process. Nowadays some organizations pilot any new application forms to confirm how easy they are to complete, and how well potential candidates actually understand them.

An application form should also clearly identify what happens in terms of taking references, and specifically at what stage of the recruitment process they will be taken, and what exactly they will be used for.

You may well be aware that some jobs advertised ask for a curriculum vitae rather than completion of an application form. In this case, the job advertisement will identify what information will be required and sometimes in what format.

As mentioned earlier, *best practice* indicates that all applications to join an organization should be acknowledged. Also, and of equal importance, each application must be treated as strictly confidential. In this context, if any recruitment data is held on computer, applicants must be advised of this fact, under the provisions of the Data Protection Act 1984.

Advertising

Any job advertisement must be clear and easily understood while being focused towards the level of applicant the organization is wishing to recruit. An advertisement is a crucial part of the recruitment process, can be very costly, and is ultimately there to attract an adequate number of suitable applicants for any job advertised.

Other features of the advertising process include:

i) An advertertisement must relate to a job that is in existence.

ii) It needs to be ensured that any suitable applicant will be considered for the vacancy advertised.

iii) As a result of the job advertisement, the recruitment process must evolve on the basis of fully endorsing equal opportunities legislation and ageism.

iv) *Best Practice* ideally leads to advertisements, and subsequent recruitment over time, ensuring a workforce that is appropriately divergent to reflect the local community and labour market. This may mean, for example, ethnic minorities and certain age groups being appropriately represented in the workforce over time.

v) A good job advertisement incorporates the following features:

   a) Identifying the specific requirements of the job and the qualifications, skills and experience that are required.

   b) A brief overview of the employing organization.

   c) Where the job is located.

   d) Details on pay and incentives.

   e) Details of any re-location packages.

   f) Whether the job is full-time, part-time, permanent or for a pre-determined period.

   g) Specific guidance as to how the application procedure will work.

Selection process

The way in which the selection process is undertaken depends primarily on what job is being offered. In addition, company policy, budget available, the skills of the personnel/recruitment team and knowledge of what is available are all factors that influence what this process looks like.

What is important is that the process itself must be there, visible, and consistent – this means that each applicant will be treated in the same way and be subject to the same selection process.

Some of the selection methods available today include:

- Interviews
- Assessment centres
- Psychometric tests and biodata.

It is likely that a selection process consists of more than one approach, and therefore the recruitment team needs to agree on the particularweighting given to each method, and in addition should ensure that each applicant is treated the same way based upon the various methods used.

The selection process also needs to follow the requirements of key legislation, which means that the selection process must, as a priority, aim to select the person most suitable for the job. Legislation in place aims to ensure the selection process is there in terms of equal opportunities, sex of the applicant, marital status of the applicant and the colour, race or ethnic origin of any applicant. Current protective legislation in this context includes the Sex Discrimination Art 1975, the Disability Discrimination Act 1995 and the Race Relations Act 1976.

The interview stage

Even with the wide range of selection methods available, it is the interview that remains the most favoured. If used, interviews should be consistently and well structured to ensure that each applicant interviewed is treated the same way, and from the organization's perspective they use the interview to maximum benefit (which means collecting specific targeted data from the interviewee).

Other areas to consider here include:

- All interviewers should be trained, have their training constantly reviewed and up-dated, and receive regular feedback on their performance, which in any case should be monitored and quality controlled.

- Each interview should be professionally conducted and consistently carried out. This means that each interview will have the same structure and have the same questions being asked.

- When used as *part* of a selection process, the interview should be used only for a specific purpose. For example, if an assessment centre is part of the selection process, it will probably include group exercises and role plays which will enable an interviewee's attributes to be assessed in a more appropriate way.

  Each interviewee should have the opportunity to ask questions. Obviously, the interviewers should be able to respond to these questions, and if not, should make a genuine commitment to *find out* and let the candidate know.

- It is at the interview stage that, usually, the interviewer will confirm each stage of the recruitment process, including details of each stage and the associated timescales. This means that the applicant will understand what happens after the interview itself, depending upon whether they have been successful at this stage.

Using references

There are two main types of referee, one who makes a character reference (a personal referee) and one who makes a statement about the candidate's ability and achievements (a business referee). Examples of a personal referee would include a teacher or a professional friend or colleague.

Almost certainly, if business references are asked for, they should include the candidate's current or most recent employer.

Usually on the application form itself, details of the requirements for references are specified, and during the selection process it must be made very clear to the candidates at what stage referees will be approached and that any information obtained from them will remain strictly confidential (the only likely exception to this will be if there is a complaint from the candidate for discrimination of some sort). Of critical importance in this part of the selection process is the validity and accuracy of the information given in the reference, and this mans that the employer must give clear and specific instructions on the reference form itself. The type of information requested will include:

- Dates (for example, to validate information given on the application form).

- Qualifications (for example, to confirm that the qualifications mentioned by the candidate on the application form are correct), job details and achievements of the candidate.

Typically, references are taken up after a job offer, which means that the job offer will be conditional on obtaining satisfactory references. Ideally, references should be obtained prior to any job offer being made.

Other issues to consider

These include:

- The whole recruitment process should be accurately documented, i.e., accurate records of the whole process should be kept.

- Strict confidentiality should be maintained at all times.

- Any unsuccessful candidate should be notified, in writing, as soon as possible.

- All candidates should have the opportunity to receive meaningful feedback on their applications.

- Any job offer letter should be made because soon as possible, because for both the successful and unsuccessful applicants delays create a poor impression of the recruiting organization, and create uncertainty. It may be the person that the organization wishes to recruit has other offers to consider also and therefore the perception of how the recruitment process is handled can be a key influencer on their final decision.

- Any job offer letter should be very carefully drafted and must detail all the terms and conditions of employment together with any specific timescale that the candidate has to accept or reject the offer, and a specified start date.

4.2 The induction process

It should be self-evident that a well-structured induction process will help a new member of staff to contribute more effectively to the business as quickly as possible.

In some ways the induction process is like a period of probation, where your new colleague undergoes a period of training, development and familiarization that all new members of staff need to go through. This period of time allows the business unit manager to judge the new entrant's suitability for the job.

The main aims of induction

- To provide suitable training for all new members of staff.

- To enable ongoing training needs to be identified.

- To improve the contribution to the business a new member of staff makes as soon as possible.

- In many cases, to record the progress and activities of a new member of staff so that, at the end of probably a six-month period, the retention or release of that new member of staff can then be confirmed or clarified (the probationary period).

Who is the induction process for?

As mentioned above, this induction training process is for all members of staff, including those brand new to the organization, and involves:

- Part-time staff.

- Those joining the organization for a limited period (contract style).

- Members of staff who are returning to work after a period of absence, (e.g., maternity leave).

Why is this process important?

- It enables a structured approach to be available which focuses on the key skills a new member of staff needs to maximize his or her contribution to the business.

- It enables early job performance to be recorded objectively and accurately so that progress can be monitored.

- It enables the team leader or supervisor to be actively involved and share in the responsibility for managing the training and development of new entrants.

The role of the business manager in the induction training process

On the first morning

Key responsibilities here include:

- To greet new members of staff when they arrive at the business unit and, as appropriate, introduce them to their team leader or supervisor.

- To give new members of staff a *tour* of the business unit, which will provide an ideal opportunity for familiarization with the premises and their new colleagues. Care needs to be exercised here, because quite possibly the new member of staff may be feeling a little apprehensive, and it must be remembered that the objective here is to make the new member of staff feel comfortable rather than be *on show*.

● To hold a meeting with the new member of staff, the team leader and possibly a member of staff who takes day-to-day responsibility for the new staff member.

The first fortnight

● Obviously ongoing support needs to be available either from the manager or from the member of staff's supervisor or team leader to ensure that he or she is able to complete all early activities.

● Early on a meeting should be held with the new member of staff to discuss terms and conditions of employment.

Areas to be covered include:

Terms

- Hours of work.

- Salary.

- Sickness.

- Any probationary period.

- The appraisal system.

- Job description.

Benefits

- Holiday allowance.

- Any organizational policies towards bonuses, and incentive schemes, for example.

- Career break.

● Either the manager or the team leader/supervisor, as appropriate, should check the progress of the new member of staff at least weekly and provide support as required.

If the new member of staff has had a team member allocated to him or her, make sure that this relationship is working in a constructive and productive way.

5

TRAINING

5.1   How individuals learn

Clearly, the way in which people benefit from training or a learning experience, or when they are being coached, for example, is largely influenced by a number of factors, one of the most important of which is the way in which they learn.

Peter Honey and Alan Mumford have tried to categorize the ways in which people do that and have considered four learning styles as follows:

The activist

An activist enjoys getting to where needed as quickly as possible, is actually a practical person and is not generally interested in all the detail. This type of learner does not enjoy repetition, and becomes quickly bored if having to consolidate learning and perhaps practise. An activist prefers to have involvement in the learning process rather than to listen or watch. This type of learner enjoys a variety of tasks or activities, enjoys the excitement of change and facing up to the unknown.

An activist is an enthusiastic individual, who enjoys being busy and revels in being in the limelight.

The reflector

This type of person when learning naturally prefers to listen and observe. A reflector usually needs time to prepare, adopts a very methodical approach and does not enjoy an experience of facing change or the unknown if having to act quickly. This category of learner requires as much detail as possible, is very orderly and does not enjoy the pressure of tight deadlines.

Therefore a reflector prefers to watch, think and consider a learning experience from as many angles as possible, gather as much data as is available, well before making any decision or drawing any conclusions. Clearly then a reflector is naturally cautious and probably prefers to work alone and adopt a low profile.

The theorist

The theorist needs to have clear objectives from any learning undertaken. This type of person needs the time to practise and often wants to practise several times before *going live*. A theorist is not comfortable in making quick decisions, and likes to be very clear about what will happen as a result, and feels very uneasy in a situation of ambiguity, change or uncertainty. A theorist often welcomes the chance to question as much as necessary in order to get the clarity required.

A theorist may well be seen to be a type of perfectionist. He or she is naturally logical in approach and self-disciplined, and looks to find ideas that are based on sound theory. The possibility of subjective judgements is very alien to a theorist and a theorist will not see acting on impulse as a possibility.

The pragmatist

This type of person enjoys a practical scenario and in a similar way to the activist is very keen to know what the outcome will be and likes to get straight to the core issues. However, the pragmatist is keen to practise after a demonstration or illustration, while enjoying working in real-life situations. The pragmatist is looking towards solutions all of the time, does not enjoy theoretically-based arguments although will enjoy problem-solving situations.

A pragmatist usually enjoys achieving aims through other people and while adopting this approach will see problems as opportunities to do even better.

When looking at training, or how to coach or mentor a member of a team, we have seen briefly how important it is to understand where an individual may be coming from. It is very important that we understand how people are feeling when they are learning, what approach it is that they will be most likely to respond to in a favourable and beneficial way.

5.2 Training

Training is an enormously complex area, and what follows highlights some of the key areas that need to be considered by any team leader, supervisor, manager or an individual who aspires to these levels of responsibility.

Who is involved in planning training and development for staff?
Individuals

Every member of a team has something to contribute here, primarily through his or her own job performance and ambitions. In today's working environment, staff are becoming increasingly used to analysing their own job performance and considering their own developmental needs. Two formal ways which are examples of how an individual may facilitate this process are through the appraisal system and their own *personal development plan*.

Team leaders/supervisors

They should be considering job cover for their own section, and be aware of the options they have, in terms of training, of how to improve their team's performance.

Managers

The management team should be able to take a *global view* of their business unit, placing ongoing day-to-day requirements with the overall business objectives and perhaps some new objectives which have not yet been made public. The various issues need to be placed in an order of priority, and the training resource devoted to addressing and supporting these issues needs to be placed in a similar order.

The advantages and disadvantages of various training and development options

Type of Training option	Advantages	Disadvantages
Face-to-face Course	- The opportunity to meet colleagues from different parts of the organization, or from other organizations. - Provides the opportunity to learn non-interrupted, away from the workplace. - The opportunity to practise new techniques in a *safe environment*. - Can be motivating. - Will focus and relate the course work to your workplace and facilitate action planning after the course.	- The post-course *high* will disappear quickly if support is not provided on return to the workplace. - Can be costly. - The timing of the face-to-face course may not be exactly when it is needed. - No managerial support.
Open-Learning Courses	- Can work at the learner's own pace. - Flexibility as to when learning takes place. - Training/learning can be undergone in smaller stages, which implies less time away from the workplace.	- Learner can be interrupted. - Easier to cancel. - Unlikely to involve group discussion. - Is very reliant upon the learner's own self-discipline and self-motivation.
Coaching	- Provides personal attention. - Provides ongoing support and guidance. - Newly learnt knowledge can be immediately practised in the work-place, and somebody will be there to ask questions and provide clarity and guidance.	- Involvement in the coaching role will take that individual away from their own job. - The coach may not be an expert! - In today's working environment of headcount constraints, may not be a practical option.

The advantages and disadvantages of various training and development options (continued)

Type of training option	Advantages	Disadvantages
Manuals, Rule Books, Guidelines	- Source of reference material that can be used by an individual at the workplace. - Consistent information available to all who refer to it. - Hopefully relatively quick to use.	- Manuals cannot answer questions. - This source of training may not contain the information that is required/needed. - Lacks the inter-personal dimension. - Can be difficult to find your way around.
Secondment	- Personal guidance from colleagues in a different section should be available. - Experience gained of working in a different environment while learning. - Opportunities available to try out new skills in a different workplace.	- The person on attachment may be seen as nuisance or interruption to the section. - Assumes coaching support is available.
Job Swap	- Can re-motivate an individual. - Will help people to understand how other people work, and the work of their section/business unit. - Will help to gain an understanding of how the different sections work together.	- Requires two or more people to want to do each other's jobs. - May impact on the output of the respective sections. - Heavy time commitment.
IT Training	- Can be done in one's own workplace. - Can be done at the learner's own pace. - Usually able to ask colleagues questions while undertaking training.	- Trainee can be easily interrupted. - Training can be postponed relatively easily. - Need for IT courses to be constantly up dated.

The previous two tables represent some of the pros and cons of different training media; no doubt you will be able to think of others. One of the key learning points from looking at the various options of training available is for you to make an informed decision about what is right either for you personally, or for your own team member when deciding how best you can support a training and learning environment in your own workplace.

Best practice before and after a training and development event

Holding a discussion before the training and development

It is to the obvious benefit of both the manager/supervisor and their team member to be very clear about why the training is about to take place.

Key aspects to consider include:

- Why the individual is going to learn something new.

- What the learner will be doing to develop skills or knowledge.

- How the learner will be able to put learning into practice back in the workplace.

- Who will be available to support the learner/trainee on return to their job (or new job, as appropriate).

- How the learner will be able to perform once he or she has had time to practise new skills or apply new levels of knowledge.

During this pre-event discussion it should be clarified what is about to be talked about because the prime objective is to ensure that the individual understands why he or she is being developed. Clearly line managers' enthusiasm and words of encouragement can make a big difference to how a person feels about this.

Holding a discussion after the training and development

Best practice would indicate that the date for this event should have been arranged at the time of the pre-event discussion. The aim would be to meet within a week of the end of the course/training event or as soon as possible after that.

Some things that are typically covered in this discussion include:

- To ask learners how they feel about the training they have received.

- The opportunity should be given to learners to ask them what they would like to discuss with you as a result of the training (for example, their action plan). Even at this early stage, learners may be in a position to discuss the progress they have made so far on applying their learning to the workplace.

- The objectives that were agreed by the learner/yourself/the trainer need to be reviewed at this discussion. Particular emphasis needs to be given on how effectively these objectives were met and to establish the reasons for this.

- It may be that the training event includes a post event *test* with the idea being to reinforce learning back in the workplace.

- Based on what was discussed prior to the training event, it now needs to be clarified what the learner will now be doing on return to the workplace in order to consolidate learning.

- It needs to be discussed and agreed what support will be available from either yourself as manager, or from a colleague to help the learner to consolidate their learning.

- Building on this, it needs to be agreed what performance levels you expect to see from the learner now and in the future (as he or she becomes more skilled) as a result of training.

- Dates should be agreed for review and progress.

- Consider the next steps.

An ongoing review of progress

In many ways the training event itself is just the beginning and the investment of time, money and other resources will be wasted unless ongoing support is available back in the business unit to consolidate and build on the learner's development.

Regular reviews of an individual's learning and progress made since the training event should be a part of life. At these (hopefully regular) review meetings, the following can be included:

- To remind each other why the development need was identified in the first place.

- To remind each other what was agreed in the post-training event de-brief, and what exactly you were both looking to see happen differently as a result.

- Do the changes, identified above, remain valid?

- A two-way discussion of how things are progressing since the training.

- It needs to be agreed whether any further support support is required.

- Is the agreed support available in practice in the workplace to facilitate the learner's consolidation of their new skills?

- Agree the next steps.

- There are plenty of training courses available and literature which will help an individual continue his or her development over the longer term.

6

MOTIVATION

6.1   Why people work

In today's working world, we are all expected to get *more out of less* (resources), where time is a crucial factor. Inevitably this means *less* in terms of quantity of effort, which means in turn there has to be an increase in the quality of effort if the equation is to balance (i.e., the desired result is to be delivered).

The question as to why people work sounds deceptively simple, as does the answer that many people give, namely, *money*.

Quite obviously in the complex working of the world of today, money is vitally important. It remains, although this may change in the future, the medium through which we obtain services and for which we *sell* our time, skills, competencies and energy. For the vast majority of the non-retired population, the way in which money is obtained on a regular basis is to go to work.

Very quickly we realize that *money* as an answer to this complex issue does not take us very far. Immediately we realize that this answer does not tell us anything about an individual's choice of work, let alone the issues relating to the workplace itself. For example, why do some members of the population choose to work in a retail outlet, while others become police officers? Why do some individuals work in the area of customer service whereas others prefer to work on a production line? Money is a key, and in some cases *the* key reason why most of us work, but it certainly is not all of the reason why we work and in particular where we work.

Social psychologists talk about *motivation* as a way for us to get a better understanding of why people work and why they exhibit certain behaviours in the workplace. The philosophy of motivation is about providing an incentive, in this context an incentive to work.

Once again, once the word incentive is mentioned, for many, money becomes the priority. The social psychologists will tell you that there are other things in every individual's mind at the same time, and not only money.

There have been a vast range of ideas written on this subject over previous centuries on why working people do the things they do. There always has been and always will be many ideas and explanations of how people have developed in the way that we have and what makes us exist and behave in particular ways both individually and in groups. Later on in this section we shall consider the ideas of some of the more influential thinkers in this area, including R.H. Maslow (Hierarchy of Needs) and Frederick Herzberg.

Motivation is an individual phenomenon, and different types of motivation occur in different situations. Each of us has needs and the things that we do at work and outside of the workplace are determined by the needs that we have. Individuals are motivated to do their best when the appropriate conditions and incentives are in place to facilitate them towards fulfilling their needs.

It can be argued that there are two main levels of individual need, as follow:

● *Basic needs*
  These include an individual's need for a *reasonable* level of salary, job security and acceptable working conditions. By fulfilling these basic needs, people can provide for the basic necessities for themselves, and if appropriate for their family.

● *High-level needs*
  A person can evolve to these higher levels only after the basic needs have been met. As such we can identify three main types of high-level needs as follows:

  a) *Acceptance needs* This is where people are accepted by others in the workplace.

  b) *Achievement needs* This is where people are doing a job which they really enjoy, matches their actual or potential levels of skill and knowledge very well and levels of performance are very encouraging.

  c) *Power needs* This is where an individual seeks to influence and possibly even control people and significant events.

As a manager or team leader, it makes logical sense to try to understand how each member of your team is motivated. By doing this you will then stand a much better chance of being able to motivate them more effectively.

Meeting the individual's basic needs

The types of behaviour that would indicate an individual being concerned about basic needs being fulfilled include: expressing concern about current levels of pay; seeking reassurance about job security; proactively looking for job clarity; raising concerns about the prevailing working conditions.

As a manager or team leader it is important that an individual's basic needs are satisfied as quickly and realistically as possible. If these basic needs are not satisfied, then individuals within your team will remain unsettled; concurrently we need to ensure that expectations are not naively raised in the process of meeting these basic needs.

Money has been traditionally the most popular way to motivate. It is also a very individual phenomenon, and research has shown that, at an individual level, once enough money is earned for *living needs* the possibility of earning more money becomes a far less significant motivator.

Although individuals clearly want to earn enough to meet their current *living needs* they also look to the future for job security so that they will be able to continue to earn enough. In today's world it is not always possible to guarantee job security indefinitely. The whole concept of the *cradle-to-the-grave* job environment has changed. Far more often these days the shape of the job market changes, individuals often work for more than one organization either by choice or by change in circumstances (for example, a business closing down or being relocated). The best approach here is to give as much reassurance to each member of your team as possible, in a way that is both honest and realistic.

The working environment and working conditions of a business vary enormously, largely dependent upon what that business actually does. The actual working environment is much more important to some than to others. In this context it is ultimately the management team working with their team members which creates a working environment that is as pleasant as possible. Undoubtedly, if working conditions are bad or unacceptable, there will be little chance of meeting the basic needs of your team.

Fulfilling the higher-level needs of your team

As we have seen acceptance needs are those needs an individual has to be accepted by other people. The types of behaviour an individual exhibits while having strong acceptance needs include: seeing the importance for having good relationships with colleagues; often seen helping out other people; likes to be involved in groups, project work and committees.

As a manager or team leader these acceptance needs can be met by some of the following activities when possible:

- Recognizing this individual's contribution.

- Arranging for this person to be involved in group activities or project work.

- Those individuals within your team having achievement needs want to do what they do to the best of their abilities. Often they like to have ongoing feedback to have the reassurance of what they are doing is being done well.

  Quite often the following additional behaviours are shown; they may be naturally competitive in nature; an individual with achievement needs takes real pride in what they do; these individuals have high levels of enthusiasm and set their own demanding targets or goals; they also work well without close supervision and want to continue with their own self development.

The team leader has a crucial role to play here in helping those members in the team that have these achievement needs. When possible the following could be done:

- Give these individuals the type of job that gives them the chance to use their abilities, and more specifically a task that can show measurable results.

- Create the environment or culture whereby these individuals can continue to develop, either through internal or external training, their ongoing level of knowledge and skills.

- While being careful with the timing, try to ensure that these individuals are given constantly more challenging pieces of work.

The members in your team with power needs will want to influence others and gain acceptance for their own views and opinions. Quite often individuals who have strong power needs are aiming to reach the higher levels of an organization. Key behaviours exhibited by these individuals include:

- A clear understanding of how an organization works and what the main aspects of internal politics are.

- Enjoys the profile of being in debates and likes to win these debates.

- Seeks to be involved in the higher-profile roles and activities whereby they have the opportunity to influence those people that matter.

- Often people with power needs value the status of any role that they have and try to demonstrate the importance of these roles.

An individual with power needs can be motivated in the following ways:

- By being given more responsibility, and on some occasions given responsibility that enables this person to have influence (on your behalf) over other members of the team.

- Possibly by preparing this individual for eventual promotion and at this new level there will be opportunities to exercise these power needs. A team leader needs to manage an individual's expectations carefully into today's world of volatile job markets.

- To enable this type of individual to be involved in some of the broader organizational activities.

The above paragraph highlights the main, although by no means all categories of a motivator.

In the case of both basic needs and high-level needs being unfulfilled, ultimately individuals may resort to leaving the organization.

Basic needs mean that levels of commitment to the organization inevitably fall. This may well have a negative affect on output or production. Clearly in this environment, to try to increase production or productivity and to manage change will become infinitely more difficult.

Again if high-level needs are not met individuals may devote their main energies to interesting activities outside of the workplace. They may spend their working day doing jobs that are below their capabilities. In some circumstances, they may become disruptive, exceed their authority, look to create their own power base and influence others in this way.

In both sets of circumstances with either sets of needs being unfulfilled, inevitably the organization will not operate as effectively as it would otherwise do.

6.2   Motivational theory

Frederick Herzberg – The motivation-hygiene theory

Herzberg completed most of his work while he was Professor of Psychology at Western Reserve University, Cleveland, and he argued that people have two different sets of needs.

Herzberg argued that traditional approaches to motivation were concerned only with the environment in which the employee worked. These basic principles involved the circumstances that surrounded an individual at the workplace, and the things the employee would be given in exchange for work. Herzberg believed that this concern with the working environment is important in managerial terms, but in itself is not sufficient for effective motivation. Herzberg believed that this other dimension requires consideration of another set of factors, those experiences which are inherent in the work itself.

Herzberg argued that work itself can be a motivator. At the time, this view was seen as a real breakthrough, as previously it had been considered necessary for management to either entice individuals to work by means of rewards or incentives, or to cajole them into working by means of various threats, or a combination of both of these methods. One of the fundamental principals of Herzberg's work was that, when a job provides an opportunity for individual and personal satisfaction for growth, a powerful new motivating force is available.

Herzberg made a distinction between hygiene factors and motivational factors.

Hygiene factors were used to describe things like working conditions, supervisory policies and practices, working relationships between teams and management, wages and reward packages. In simple terms these hygiene factors were there to meet most of the *basic needs* that we mentioned earlier that were traditionally thought by management to effect motivation in totality. Herzberg developed this principle of hygiene factors because he saw them as being essentially *preventative* actions – this meant that the hygiene factors were there to remove sources of potential dissatisfaction from the working environment rather than to be motivators in themselves. An inadequate level of hygiene factors will lead, according to this argument, to a less than fully effective workforce, while hygiene factors at an acceptable level will merely create an ongoing status quo rather than a *net gain* situation.

In his work, Herzberg uses the term motivation to describe an individual's feeling of achievement, of personal growth and recognition that will be available in jobs that offer sufficient challenge and potential to develop the employee.

In the context of these theories, one of Herzberg's guiding principles was that he considered apathy and minimum effort as being the natural result of jobs that offer the employee no more satisfaction than regular pay and a decent work environment. *Hygiene factors* may well keep employees from complaining, although concurrently they will not want to make employees work harder or more efficiently than absolutely necessary. This is why Herzberg saw pay and benefits to be hygiene factors. In his research Herzberg concluded that the main effect of pay and reward is to create potential levels of dissatisfaction among employees (when pay and reward is perceived as inadequate) and that the principal effect of an increase in pay and reward to remove these levels of dissatisfaction rather than to create satisfaction.

Herzberg's hygiene factors could be argued to correspond to the needs identified at the lower end of Maslow's *hierarchy of needs* and in a similar way Herzberg's *motivating factors* could relate to those needs of the upper part of the triangle.

Maslow's hierarchy of needs is illustrated below:

Figure 6.1: Hierarchy of needs

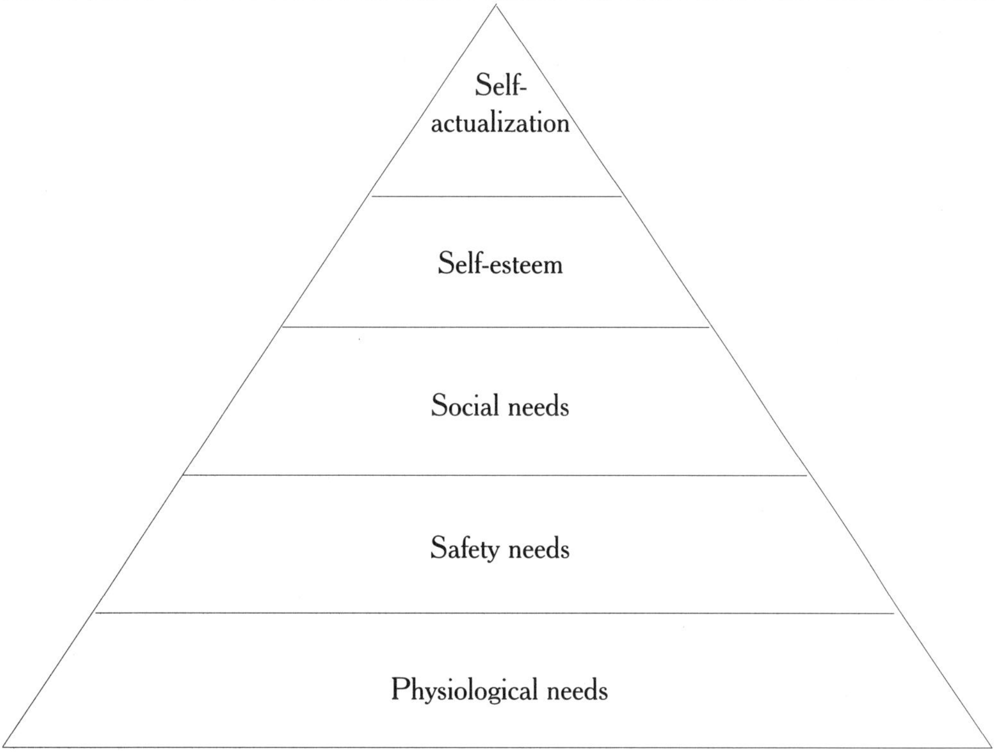

The dotted line across Maslow's hierarchy indicates the possible *break point* when we compare his views to those of Herzberg. Those above the dotted line relate to the motivating factors, and those below to the hygiene factors.

Broadly, using Maslow's model, the physiological safety and some element of social needs relate to the requirements of an employee to have job security, a favourable working environment, supportive organizational personnel policies, a regular salary and job security. Towards the middle of this triangle, as an individual employee heads up the hierarchy, interpersonal relations with colleagues (management, for example) become more important.

Above the dotted line, the motivating factors for an individual employee revolve around the nature of the work itself and how an individual can be motivated by completing a particular piece of work. Towards the higher levels of the hierarchy, an individual employee is motivated by having (and actively seeking) more responsibility in the workplace, and welcomes (and expects) more recognition for what they do. In addition, particularly towards the apex of the triangle, individuals are looking for opportunities to advance and develop their career.

With reference to Maslow's hierarchy of needs, each individual employee will begin at the bottom and will evolve to the next stage only when the previous level of motivational needs have been fulfilled. For each individual employee, it is likely that each level on the hierarchy will mean different things, and each individual will move up (and potentially back down) the hierarchy at different speeds and for different reasons. In today's working environment, reasons for moving up and down the hierarchy could include: change of job; promotion; being made redundant; being appointed to manager projects; moving into a new set of offices.

David McClennand also did some work on an individual's needs to achieve. He argued that, along with all the other motivational factors, this need to achieve could vary considerably among individual employees and would be influenced by the following factors:

- The level of satisfaction an individual can obtain from achieving is derived mainly from the act of achieving itself, rather than from any other external rewards (primarily financial reward).

- Individual employees proactively want to assume responsibility for achieving a particular task or tasks that they are expected to achieve.

- Often individual employees look to set realistic achievement goals which involve calculated risks. Tasks that are too easy to accomplish, for the individual employee with high achievement needs, are avoided because they do not present enough of a challenge. Also, McClennand argued, responsibilities that are considered to be too difficult are also avoided because the individual perceives that the probabilities of success are too low.

- Individuals who look to fulfill their achievement need have a need for ongoing and specific feedback in order that guidance can be received as to how well (or otherwise) they have done. These types of individuals do always want to be aware of how they are progressing against their targets or objectives.

Another dimension in McClennand's work was about an individual employee's affiliation needs. These affiliation needs can be correlated to the social needs on Maslow's hierarchy of needs.

McClennand saw an affiliation need as being very different from an achievement need, arguably the opposite. The high-affiliation employee places a great deal of importance upon human relations, both in terms of being with and getting on with other people. McClennand's research suggested that an individual employee with high affiliation needs would have the following characteristics:

- One who would derive greater satisfaction from the people he or she worked with, rather than from the work itself.

- Contrary to high achievers, high affiliates tend not to respond as well to specific and ongoing feedback about their progress in their particular role. Typically they respond more favourably to compliments from others about their attitude towards their work, and how valuable they are to the organization.

- High affiliates probably make decisions about their job preferences or even career path on the basis of who they will be working with and for, rather than on the nature of the work itself. In extreme cases, these high affiliates, given the choice, would let their work suffer should that task's achievement conflict in any way with the need to be accepted or well regarded by their colleagues.

- A high affiliate tends to prefer a role with high prestige rather than a job that demands excellence of performance.

- Again contrary to the high achiever, the act of achieving is itself not as motivating to the high affiliate. This means that a high affiliate will be much less likely to want to accept demanding levels of personal responsibility.

When drawing conclusions from his work, McClennand did not see affiliation needs and achievement needs as necessarily being mutually exclusive. How these two needs apply will vary, to some extent, for each individual employee. It may well be that a given individual employee could have some of all of the motives mentioned above. What is clear, however, is that a manager or team leader needs to treat a high achiever very differently from a high affiliate.

7

MANAGING A GROUP

7.1   Leading a team

In this section we need to be clear about the differences we refer to when discussing a group and a team. In general terms within a group individuals tend to work more independently, taking responsibility for their own (independent) tasks. Within a team, there may well tend to be more cooperation, a sharing of responsibilities and reliance on each other.

Some characteristics of a group

- A tendency for more formal communication to take place.

- Probably less *free expression*.

- People within the group do not expect to receive support from elsewhere within the group.

- It is more likely that an individual will not know what other individuals are doing and how they contribute to the overall progress of the group.

- Because of the emphasis on a more formal communication structure, it is possible that within a group any disagreement *may* become hostile, surpressed or even avoided.

- The goals and objectives of the group are likely to be more imposed rather than discussed and agreed.

- Individuals in the group do not always know what the overall group/team objectives are.

Characteristics of a team

- Usually, individuals within a team knowingly work towards a common goal or set of objectives and realize how important their contribution is to overall success.

- Communication can be a combination of both formal and informal approaches – in this environment, individuals feel more *free* to say what they feel.

- There tends to be much more interdependence within a team, with individuals taking and giving support.

- More often than not, individuals within a team are aware of each other's tasks and objectives, and are more aware of the overall team's/business unit's objectives.

- There is a tendency towards more open and two-way constructive feedback.

- Individuals within a team are more likely to feel *empowered* to achieve their own objectives and knowing how these then contribute to overall success.

- Generally, within a team all team members are consulted and involved in establishing the team's objectives.

- Individual ideas and contributions are both welcomed and recognized. There is a recognition that a *blame culture* should be avoided.

Please note the points above are some themes and ideas and are not intended to be an exhaustive and general list of characteristics distinguishing between a group and a team. Clearly there are other influences, for example:

- The type of business within which a group or team operates.

- The management/leadership style of the team leader.

- The length of time the business unit has been running.

- The purpose of the group or team.

The role of a team leader

A team leader has a key role in deciding which direction the team is to go in, in confirming which business goals or objectives are priorities, and how success will be defined. In this respect, a team leader must be able to share the *vision* of what success will look like in the future, and then be able to verbalize how in more specific terms the team will get there. Being motivational to maximize the business contribution of each member of the team is a key attribute of a successful team leader, as is the ability to mould the collection of individuals into a team which can, together, deliver more with greater success.

Some qualities of an effective leader

Most of us believe that each of us has some leadership qualities and that it is possible for all of us to develop these qualities with support, guidance and practice.

The ability to make good decisions (the definition of a good decision varies significantly according to what type of decision we are talking about) is a very important attribute to an effective team leader. The thought process for making decisions can be outlined as follows:

- Consider what you are trying to achieve.

- Discuss and agree objectives (that is your desired outcome(s)). At this stage it is important to consider who else may have to be involved, for example, line management and/or colleagues.

- Be aware of what internal and external factors may affect your decision.

- Try to get all the information that you will need to make an informed decision.

- Consider what options are available to you, all of which must be realistic and cost effective. It may be at this stage that you realize more information is required.

- Decide upon an effective way of comparing each of these options, probably against the same set of agreed criteria.

- Either alone, or involving line management and/or colleagues, consider how to select the *best* option.

- After this debate, select which option is considered to be the best way to proceed.

- Communicate the decisions to all interested parties. These may include line management, colleagues, peers, other departments, and so on.

- A leader also needs to have utmost integrity, which means that the promises that are made are kept, that you are seen to lead by example, and that favouritism is never a feature of your leadership style. Good leaders are seen as tough but fair. Any business unit head or team leader ensures that the team always feels challenged and stretched by the objectives which are agreed. On every occasion a team effectively led feels fully involved in developing these challenging objectives and therefore feels more empowered and a part of the tasks which are set to be achieved. In the context of these demanding targets or objectives, which are inevitable these days in any case, a team should be resourced as effectively as possible (again, in a climate of relentless cost constraints and resource scarcity).

The working environment of ongoing and rapid change is effecting all of us, and a leader must be able to show the ability to be flexible and adaptable in this prevailing work climate. Teams will be less than effective when they are unclear about what the eventual objectives are, and they are not comfortable with why these goals and objectives are in place. Change is also resisted when the benefits of what they are doing are unclear and that each team member does not understand what he or she may gain from change in the first place. Some individuals may disagree with the change, although throughout a leader should ensure that all team members know and understand what is expected of them. Through this time of change, a leader will be able to clearly illicit and communicate the team's objectives. Regular explanations need to be given as to why the change or changes are necessary. Concurrently the whole team needs to be aware what the probable benefits of the change will be, and what challenges will be faced along the way (if known!). Quite often, a leader will divide an overall rate of change into several smaller phases to make each of these smaller phases appear more durable – this approach has the added benefit of helping each individual in the team become more comfortable with what they are doing and why in the shorter term.

None of us have an infinite knowledge of anything, and each of us can always learn from our colleagues in the workplace. A team leader is no different and one of the ways in which this can be done is by being a good listener. A good listener is able to promote an ongoing exchange of information within a team and this in itself will help to establish and build relationships. Some of the behaviours involved in being an effective listener include:

- Encouraging others to communicate with you.
- *Concentration*.
- Taking notes where necessary.
- Resisting the temptation to interrupt.
- Responding appropriately on each occasion.

It will always be the case that the team leader will have ultimate responsibility for the team's performance. This involves constant responsibility for the team's success in meeting business targets, the reasons why a team does not meet business targets, for each of your team members performance and for each individual team member's successes. In this scenario, as a team leader there is no-one else to look for to blame, there is nowhere to hide, and this aspect of responsibility without doubt comes with the territory.

A team leader will not always be liked in the sense of being the most popular member in a team, but should always be respected. Respect can also be earned by a team leader being genuinely interested in his or her team members. A good team leader will be able to talk on a *one-to-one* basis to each member of the team, show a real interest and understanding about what they do, how well (or not) they perform, and what contribution each of their team makes to the success of the business unit. Also, and not necessarily work related, a team leader can make a big difference to an individual if he or she remembers something important, which may be small in itself, but huge in significance. For example, a birthday, anniversary, school sports day, and so on.

There will be times when the going will get very tough and challenges may seem insurmountable. It is on these occasions that a good team leader is able to remain calm. How a team leader responds to a crisis, and is seen by his team responding to a crisis, will determine to a very large extent how they respond. A team inevitably looks to the team leader for guidance and leadership during a time of crisis. Generally, a good leader is not one who is seen only annually at the work Christmas party. A leader therefore needs to be visible and accessible and obviously a balance needs to be achieved between being there for your team, and carrying out the other responsibilities which a team leader has. *Best practice* is a concept, introduced by Hewlett Packard some years ago, now called *MBWA* (management by walking about) which occurs when a team leader walks around an office or business unit and talks to the team members in a relaxed, informal and sometimes unstructured way. This means the team leader is getting a real *feel* for what is happening within the team. This visibility and investment in taking the time to talk to a team will pay dividends. The team leader will then be seen as somebody who is both accessible and approachable, someone whom team members can go to, discuss issues, problems, concerns or make suggestions.

Finally, a team leader can often add most value when looking for practical solutions to challenges and problems. Quite often, it is common sense and a practical approach will be the best way forward, as not only will this make more sense but will also work best in the workplace. We have all seen team leaders who are experts in theory, but show little understanding of what these theories mean in practical terms. A team leader in this respect will take a more logical approach and think around an issue before implementing any *knee-jerk* reaction. A team leader here will look for a logical and simple as possible way to proceed and as we have mentioned above; the need to involve the team throughout remains essential.

It is often helpful to look at ourselves and consider what attributes we have as a potentially effective team leader and similarly what areas we need to concentrate upon in order to develop. One way of doing this is by highlighting our strengths and developmental areas under four sections on a chart, as follows:

Figure 7.1

Strengths (What we know we can do well and have the evidence to prove it)	Developmental Areas (What we know we need to work on – again having specific examples to work on)
Opportunities (What opportunities are available to help you to develop – this could be training, finding a mentor, obtaining a transfer)	Threats (What may prevent you from succeeding and developing – could be cost constraints, possible redundancy, not having the support of your line manager)

By completing a self-review like this, you will be able to highlight what strengths you have, and what you need to work on. You can then select, say, two or three priority areas which may be strengths (making us stronger) or specific developmental areas and then produce a realistic and achievable action plan which will detail what you intend to do to facilitate your own self-development. There is, no doubt, the drive to achieve self-development, and the responsibility for doing this is with individuals themselves ... that is you!

Gaining credibility as a leader

There are many ways of considering how credibility may be earned in a leadership position, and we shall consider three:

● The power of a personality.

● Role competence.

- The power of your position as team leader.

Logically then each of these dimensions may change in terms of the proportions to which they apply, and the balance of these three dimensions will vary according to the particulars of any situation.

A personality can be very important because it is a key factor in determining the role a team leader has with the team, and also line management and peers. As ever, the *right* personality is very difficult to define although some of the more critical aspects are as follows:

- A more *positive* personality tends to mean:

    a) Effective relationship-building with the team, line management and peers.

    b) The team leader appearing confident (even if you are not!).

    c) Portraying a positive attitude.

    d) Could well enhance the two-way communication process within a team.

    e) Helps to facilitate a genuine level of interest and concern for your team members.

    f) Will create an environment where team member's opinions are welcomed, respected and valued.

- Some *pitfalls* to be aware of when considering a team leader's personality are:

    a) A team leader will not be successful relying wholly on personality.

    b) A too powerful personality can become overbearing for the team members.

    c) A too positive personality can lead to overoptimism and naivety.

    d) Failing to be sincere when requesting people's views and opinions and failing to listen to them or act upon them.

There is still a highly held view that if a team leader knows every aspect of each of the team member's roles, and can do, or has done each of these roles themselves, this will be crucial in establishing and subsequently enhancing their credibility.

When a team leader is in a position of having significant levels of knowledge and proven capability in terms of what the business unit is setting out to achieve, it will then be possible for the team leader to:

- Share knowledge with the team which should facilitate team performance and individual self-development.

- To build on this sound level of knowledge and continually keep up to date.

- Show to your team that you are not *foolproof* and may make mistakes like everybody else.

- Ensure that, as team leader, you show a genuine interest in how your team members are enhancing their own levels of knowledge.

- Never assume that you know everything; somebody somewhere knows at least as much as you!

- As a team leader, you should take sensible opportunities to demonstrate your knowledge or skill.

- The level of knowledge or skill that you hold will enable you to become a mentor or coach for some members of your team. The dangers of a team leader with much knowledge are quite clear, and potentially dangerous to the team's performance.

- A team leader may try to keep knowledge secret and not be prepared to share it with the team.

- The team leader may assume the role of being absolutely perfect.

- There is a clear risk of being seen as the office *know-all* and using knowledge as a way of putting down team members.

Position power or role power is a part of the job that a team leader does – it is there for all to see. By implication then, the team leader's role gives implied authority to the person assuming that role. This position power can be used to facilitate the structure and direction of a team, and to provide ongoing reassurance to each team member. This position power also allows a team leader to act clearly as a role model. There is no reason for this position power to allow the team leader to become dictatorial in any way, or to take advantage and bully individuals.

Being a team leader is always challenging, and there is an inherent need to be positive at all times. This in itself can be very difficult, particularly when, for example, bad news may have to be delivered or you are not feeling quite yourself that day or you have just heard some bad news. How, in fact, you perceive yourself as a team leader and how your team perceive you as a team leader may be quite similar, more often than not; however, your view and their view can be quite different and furthermore these differences once highlighted come as a complete surprise to the team leader. There are some fairly easy ways to begin the process of understanding how you see yourself as a team leader and how others see you. Below is an example of a simple questionnaire that could be completed by yourself and each of your team members and the results compared. Ideally, these results would serve as the basis of an open and frank discussion about you as a team leader – you will see that this example of questionnaire is not very detailed and could be used merely as a starting point in any discussion that follows; specific examples to illustrate any points could be discussed (and this should be encouraged).

Table 7.1

Attribute	Always	Sometimes	Never
Positive			
Enthusiastic			
Decisive			
Sense of humour			
Confident			
Business focused			
High levels of energy			

For a team member or team members to complete the questionnaire is merely an indication of what could and should become a very fruitful and positive working relationship. These self-reviews and team leader questionnaires should be completed at regular intervals and, over time, will help facilitate a positive two-way communication structure, based on an open and honest working environment where everybody can say what they feel without fear of recrimination. As the recipient of such *upward feedback* there is a clear need to have *broad shoulders*. It is all too easy to become sensitive and self-defensive when receiving feedback from your team members that is less than complimentary. As a team leader you need to try to understand why your team members are saying what they are saying, because usually they have a very good reason for doing so. Try to let them explain their feelings and their points of view, when possible, giving specific examples to support their opinions. Again, a team leader should be, and be seen to be, receptive to these views and to take the opportunity to value the opinions of your team and to learn from them.

Leadership styles

Leadership styles are considered in greater detail elsewhere, although in the context of leading a team it is important that some of the key principles are outlined below. Every team leader will have an individual and slightly different leadership style – although there will be some clear general characteristics that will be drawn across some main leadership styles, as we shall see. Examples of such styles are autocratic, dictatorial and participative. Each of us has a preferred leadership style, that is the style to which we naturally allude. There will be some circumstances in which our own preferred leadership style is the most effective one to use, and others where a more different style may be appropriate. All team leaders need to be aware of the most appropriate and effective leadership style to use according to the situation with which they are faced – but changing your leadership style is not as simple as changing your socks! It can be quite complex and the starting point is to have a clear understanding of what your leadership style is, and how it can be changed. Some team leaders are able to change styles quite naturally and seamlessly and seem to adapt very easily to every situation which they need to manage. Others try to apply their one favoured leadership style to every situation even though they may be faced with some scenarios in which this approach will just not work.

An outline of some of the main leadership styles is as follows:

Autocratic

These team leaders believe, without doubt, that they are the boss and will adopt *a tells style* towards their team. They believe that their team needs to be dictated to, people only respond to strict discipline and are almost totally driven by results. As a result, it is very probable that their team feels excluded and demotivated.

Participative

This type of team leader proactively welcomes and encourages contributions from the team members. Throughout the team leader tries to consult their feelings to obtain their involvement in any initiative and tries to maximize their contribution towards achieving business objectives. One potential danger here is that the team leader effectively abandons (sometimes unintentionally) control to the team. If this leadership style works well, then teams feel involved, empowered and very motivated.

Democratic

Again, as with the participative style, this type of team leader encourages the involvement of the team and often transfers control and the ability (and authority although never ultimate authority) to make decisions to the team itself. Usually, the team leader adopting a democratic style manages by consensus. There is a real risk by adopting this style that a team will lose focus on the primary objective of meeting business targets.

Laissez-faire

This type of team leader just does not get involved at all, and lets the team run by itself. He or she does not want to get involved in managing any issues or in resolving any conflicts that may arise. While the team itself *may* in the short term think this approach is wonderful, it will probably lead to the team lacking any real direction towards achievements.

Building a positive working environment

A team leader must try to create a working atmosphere that is conducive to success and to each of the team members contributing to the maximum of their capabilities. There are some immediate ways in which a team leader can facilitate this progress:

a) Recognizing success – this can be done by praising individual team members in public, and organizing and hosting team events. In addition each of your team members needs to have regular performance reviews so that they are clearly aware of how well they are doing against agreed individual objectives – this also means that they know that their boss (i.e., you!) are very interested in how they are getting on and know how well they are doing. Within the constraints of reality (probably budget!) reward outstanding contributions when possible – at the very least ensure that as team leader you are aware that these outstanding contributions have been made and take the trouble to say "well done" and "thank you".

b) Always act with integrity – the basis of this aspect of reflective team leadership is communicating at all times honestly, regularly, and with everybody. It is essential that a team leader keeps any promises and maintains any commitments that have been made. In this context, it is never wise to ask a team member to do anything that you as team leader would not be prepared to do yourself. This also means that a team leader needs to be seen to act fairly with customers, which includes team members (as some of the team leader's internal customers) and external customers.

c) Facilitate a working environment where open communication is a way of life – this environment can be created by holding regular meetings and open forums, MBWA (mentioned earlier), being accessible and available to your team members while encouraging a two-way flow of communication at every opportunity.

d) Establishing and building effective relationships – every team member should be able to voice views and opinions, which as we have already mentioned need to be welcomed, valued and acted upon as appropriate. Any areas of potential conflict should be resolved by the team leader before the issue becomes too serious and destructive. In fact, building positive relationships both between the team leader and the team members themselves will encourage everybody to support each other and will minimize the rise of a *blame culture* evolving during times of conflict.

e) Day-to-day actions – this involves ensuring that each of your team members knows not only what their day-to-day responsibilities are, but also what exceeding these responsibilities looks like. Effective leadership is all about inspiring your team members to exceed expectations, both their own and those of the business. A working environment of continuous improvement, *getting it right first time*, cooperation, and quality of service has to be created, no mean feat in itself. This also means there must be a way of recognizing success and the way this can be done depends on what is realistic within each organization. Some may have an *employee of the month*, where others will be able to recognize success in a much more tangible way, with a bonus or holiday.

f) Acceptance of responsibility – within this working environment of each team member striving for excellence, the team leader needs to ensure that all team members are absolutely clear about what it is they need to be doing and how they need to approach their duties. In addition, the importance of the way in which each team member's activities impact and interact with the others needs to be made very clear. Over time, it may be possible to increase the responsibilities that each of your team members has, although the rate at which this is done must be realistic according to the abilities and desires of each team member.

Motivating a team

Some theories of motivation are considered elsewhere, we shall here merely highlight some of the important areas in the context of leading a team effectively.

A team leader needs to realise that each of the team members is an individual. This means that they will be motivated in a different way and possibly for different reasons. Some motivators include:

- Pay.
- The possibility of career progression.
- Pride in one's work.
- Working with a team.
- Enjoying a challenge.
- Gaining increased responsibility.
- Achieving promotion.
- Being coached and developed.

In any case, an effective team will be constantly being developed by its team leader and this in itself should provide a motivational working environment. At the very least, the team will be constantly gaining new knowledge and developing new skills which in turn should help overall business performance constantly improve. An added bonus here is that the provision of coaching and ongoing support and development need not be expensive.

Setting and agreeing business objectives

A team needs to know where it is going, what it is it needs to be doing to meet (and hopefully exceed) the required levels of business performance.

In this respect, an effectively run team is constantly focused on the goals for which they are aiming and which they will have been involved in creating. A team leader, whenever possible, involves the whole team in discussing what needs to be achieved, and how collectively they can strive to meet these targets and objectives. Usually, if a team has been involved in discussing and agreeing what goals they need to aim for, they have commitment throughout while working to achieve them.

A business objective usually needs to be:

- Specific – this means it is very clear to every member of the team what it is that needs to be done.

- Demanding – this means the challenges set will be stretching and tough. In today's working world this is the same everywhere, but nevertheless, they should be something that can be seen as achievable.

- Measurable – this means everybody in the team understands that what they are doing can be measured, and therefore ongoing progress towards the overall business goals can be recorded and monitored.

- Roles and responsibilities – these need to be discussed with every member of the team so that each member knows what he or she needs to contribute to the successful meeting of business objectives.

- Communication – throughout the team leader, specifically, and the team members themselves will have their business objectives at the forefront of their minds. Regular communication about what these objectives are, and how progress is being made, is essential.

7.2   How a team can work

A team can be defined as "a group of up to ten people who rely on each other to reach a common purpose or goal".

Elements of such a team include:

- Each member of the team works towards a common purpose, to achieve some agreed objectives or aims.

- Each member of this team needs to be given ongoing support.

- Undoubtedly each member of the team will be dependent upon the others to do the job and to collectively achieve the task expected.

Within each team, there will be *norms*. Norms are a team's unwritten rules about how team members should behave and conduct themselves.

Examples of team *norms* include:

- Dress code.

- Attitude to flexibility, for example, hours of work and days of work.

- Views on lunchtime activities.

- Attitude to office or business unit tidiness.

- The way in which each team member is expected to interact with the others. As a general rule, *norms* will be slightly different for each team, although they are critically important because they help to bind a team together. Group *norms* can be very powerful and can sometimes complement overall business objectives and on occasion can be counter-productive. In this respect, any business unit manager must look to amend, if this is ever appropriate, any group *norm* with care and sensitivity. Within the group itself, *norms* are usually changed only after they have been brought out into the open and discussed in full.

Roles within a team

Meredith Belbin produced a model that indicated the various roles that should be fulfilled within a team in order for that team to work to its optimum capacity. Typically individuals naturally allude to a preferred role and look to fulfill this role within a team. If this is not possible, there may be instances of conflict within a team whereby two individuals are vying with each other for one particular role. Alternatively, an individual may adapt quite nicely to a secondary role which they may turn out to be equally as good at. Should this not be the case, it is possible for an individual to become disruptive, negative, suffer a fall in personal morale or even exit the group.

Belbin outlined the following roles:

- *Chairman* – usually an individual with an objective viewpoint having a leading role in achieving a team's objectives.

- *Shaper* – this person will be key influencer, often extrovert and impatient for success and for progress to be made.

- *Plant* – a naturally creative and intelligent team member looking to *invent* different solutions to facilitate progress towards group objectives. Often a visionary and would not see details or line of authority as being important.

- *Resource investigator* – somebody who responds to a challenge, who may find it difficult to sustain interest, while being enthusiastic and inquisitive.

- *Monitor evaluator* – continually reviews the progress of the team as it heads toward meetings its business objectives. A reliable member of the team, who will look to monitor progress against agreed *milestones*.

- *Completer/finisher* – an orderly individual who likes to see things through to the end. Will sometimes be wary of change and prefer a working environment of continuity.

- *Team worker* – a social member of the team who always promotes team spirit and the social aspect of team activity.

- *Company worker* – an individual who is hardworking, organized, structured in his or her approach to their duties and likes regularity in ongoing work activities.

- *Specialist* – an individual who may well be seconded to a team for specialist knowledge or input, probably for a shorter period of time.

Each of us knows which of these roles we would normally prefer to do. Ideally, we would obtain the role that suits us best, although in reality it may be that we would either need to adapt to a slightly different role, or even be asked to change role depending on the resources available to the unit head or team leader at that time. Flexibility is an inherently positive trait for an effective team leader, and effective team member.

The evolution of a team

It is argued that teams, like individuals, have a predictable, at least in terms of stages (and not timescale), life cycle. If a unit manager or team leader can be clear where a team is in terms of this life cycle, management styles or leadership styles and behaviours can be adapted accordingly. The five stages of this life cycle model, introduced by Tuckman, are as follows:

- *Forming* – this is where a group of individuals who are to form a team come together. This may be the first time that this group of people have met, some may know each other, while some may be complete strangers to everybody else. Essentially then the team at this stage is still a group of individuals. Most interaction within the team concerns the early stages of relationship building and for some individuals to try and *jockey* for their preferred positions and to try to stamp their identity on the group. From the team leader's perspective, focus upon the task in hand or team objectives must always be facilitated.

- *Storming* – at this stage individuals within the team try to obtain their preferred role. It is quite possible at this stage some conflict may emerge, and this conflict needs to be managed. At this stage it is vital for the team leaders to focus on the issues to be managed rather than on personalities. Also some individuals within a team will confidently work their way through this storming stage, particularly if they have achieved the role to which they aspired. Others may well feel more vunerable, facing the prospect of a different role or activity, not having made any friends within the group, and feeling particularly insecure.

- *Norming* – the group then evolves to a stage of regular working patterns, agreed ways of having discussions, making decisions and agreeing the ways ahead. Communication tends to be more open and working relationships become more established. The team leader needs to build on this stage, identifying clearly any areas for concern and discussing them in an open environment, and ensuring most, if not all, of the individual team members are feeling comfortable in the roles that they are now asked to take.

- *Performing* – it is at this stage, according to Tuckman's philosophy, that this group of people perform to their maximum capacity. Clearly, the team leader seeks to maintain this maximum level of performance for as long as possible.

- *Mourning* – this is where the period of optimum performance has passed and depends on many different factors. For example, the specifics of the task being pursued, the culture within which the team operates, the leadership or management style of the team leader, the energy within the team, and the period of time involved.

Other guiding principles of Tuckman's models include that if a new team member arrives or an existing team member departs then the group as a whole will go back to the forming stage.

Although Tuckman proposes a four-stage model leading to optimum group performance (i.e., prior to the mourning stage) this may take a considerable period of time. In reality, a business is effectively seen to perform immediately, irrespective of where it may be in terms of its evolution according to Tuckman's model.

Most teams begin to take care of themselves and encourage each other, agree their own *norms* for resolving conflict, and are aware of, value, respect and acknowledge each other's contributions.

Ideally, in a team environment everybody listens to each other and the team works in an environment where ideas are encouraged, recognized and valued. Everybody within that team operates towards a common goal or business objective. Care needs to be taken to ensure that individuals within the team do not begin to operate on their *own agenda*, because this can lead to conflict, even hostility and a breakdown of trust within the team. Alternatively, beware of the scenario where no-one in a team is prepared to take responsibility for either his or her own actions or those of colleagues. These circumstances are not conducive to optimum performance and are symbolized by a working environment where communication within the team is not as effective as it could be and that relationships within the team are not as powerful as they potentially should be.

7.3   Meetings

These days meetings take up a significant amount of our time. A meeting should always be seen to benefit in some way those who attend, and to have some positive influence on their business. Far too often this is not the case, and most of us will have had many experiences of attending meetings which seem long, boring, badly planned, lack direction, and all in all are quite a painful experience.

Obviously the timing of a meeting is very important and those that last for hours, and sometimes days, are clearly too long! Often, meetings of around 30 minutes can be very effective because everybody should have the chance to contribute in a focused way, there is no opportunity to waste time, and due to this emphasis on a fairly short period of time, attendees have to focus on agreeing actions and making decisions.

There are many, many ways in which meetings can go wrong. Some of the more common reasons for meetings being ineffective include:

- The meetings last too long.
- Team members having to attend meetings unnecessarily.
- Team members attending meetings without clear objectives.
- Agendas being dominated by the manager or team leader.
- The meeting itself not having an agenda or an agenda that is unrealistic or badly structured.
- The meeting has an ineffective chairperson.

- The absence of a time-keeper to make sure that the meeting runs to time.

There are, however, ways in which all of us can work at improving the meetings we have responsibility for organizing. We shall discuss some of these possibilities later on and these will include:

- Developing the skills of the chairperson.

- Preparing the agenda.

- Regularly getting feedback on the meetings that are held within the business unit.

- Involving the relevant members of the team in the meetings that are held.

Organizing a meeting

The first thing to establish is to be very clear why the meeting is being held. What is the end objective from holding this meeting and what are the specific objectives that are looking to be achieved? Undoubtedly, all meetings need a focus because it is very important that the temptation to have an irrelevant and tangential debate is avoided.

When you are organizing a meeting, the number of people attending is often determined by the practicalities of any one business unit. It would be ideal for somewhere between 4 and 12 people. If a business unit has more than 12 people in it, it may be that the meeting itself could be split into two smaller meetings. Alternatively, an agenda could be arranged in a particular way to give all members within a team the chance to attend, over time on a rotational basis. A further option is to create sub-groups within a business unit that could work on particular and relevant issues before and after the meeting. This means many more people have the chance to be directly involved in the meeting itself.

Long meetings are deadly. In fact some short meetings can be deadly! Whenever possible, a meeting should not really last more than two hours, although again in reality this may not be possible for practical reasons. If meetings are being organized and the attendees have to travel significant distances, possibly involving overnight stays, then costs alone will mean that the business will need to obtain *value* from this event. One indication of this could well be an *all-day* meeting. Quite often, a meeting lasting half an hour will be most effective. If a team leader deliberately wants to *limit* the time of the meeting in this way, it could be scheduled 30 minutes before lunch or 30 minutes before the end of the day! This approach undoubtedly focuses the minds of those in attendance.

When organizing a meeting, usually the chairperson or the nominee has responsibility for sending out the agenda, together with any preliminary background information.

The agenda

An agenda should usually have the following features:

- Identify the proposed start and finish times.

- Give a time for each agenda item.

- Identify who is responsible for covering each item on the agenda.

- Clarify why each item is on the agenda.

- Identify the desired outcome from having each item on the agenda.

- Should arrive on each attendee's desk at least 48 hours prior to the meeting itself.

One possible layout for an agenda is as follows:

Agenda item	Sponsor	Topic	Desired outcome	Duration of agenda item
1				
2				
3				
4				
5				

Some additional thoughts for creating an effective agenda include:

- Ensure that the more demanding items on the agenda are covered early on, when all attendees are at their most alert.

- Probably put the most important items to be covered towards the middle of the agenda. This means that they are covered when the meeting is well underway, and also enables any late comers to be fully involved at the most critical part of the meeting. Try to end each meeting covering an issue that all attendees agree on. The aim of doing this is to unify the group at the end of the meeting prior to departure.

The chairperson

The chairperson has a crucial role in determining the effectiveness of a meeting. Some of the chairperson's key responsibilities include:

- Organizing the meeting itself. This aspect includes time-keeping, taking notes, and organizing the logistics of the venue, room, refreshments, etc.

● Facilitating the meeting itself. This means all discussions are kept moving, regular summaries are included as part of the meeting, all attendees have the chance to be involved in the meeting, and that clear ground rules for the meeting are established at the outset.

● Effectively ensuring that all attendees are involved in a fair way. This means that there will be times when the more talkative attendees need to be controlled and the quieter attendees encouraged to make their contribution.

● There will be occasions when conflict needs to be handled by the chairperson, who throughout must remain impartial and in control.

In effect, the chairperson need not do all of the work. For example, an attendee could be nominated to *time keep*. Somebody else could (and probably should) take the minutes. Possibly another attendee could be invited to regularly summarize the progress made throughout the meeting.

An effective chairperson should be capable in steering discussions. This means attendees having the opportunity to share what they know and to express the opinions that they have. This should eventually lead to some agreement on the proposed courses of action and eventually making a decision. There may be times when a discussion needs to be halted or deferred. Possibly all the information that is required to make a decision is not available, a key person who is crucial to the decision in question may be absent from the meeting, or it is appropriate that the meeting takes more time to think a particular issue through.

The minutes of a meeting

The minutes of a meeting are a formal record of the meeting itself. They are very important when attendees need to be formally reminded of the action points that they are responsible for and if a record of the meeting has to be circulated to non-attendees.

Usually, minutes contain the following key features:

● The time, date and place of the meeting.

● A list of who chaired the meeting, together with who actually attended, and who was unable to attend.

● Identify the agenda items and their outcomes.

● Outline the main arguments put forward by each agenda item. Sometimes in this narrative, the individuals who made various points are identified, and sometimes not.

● The minutes need to highlight those individuals who have specific responsibility to take action as a result of particular agenda items.

● Identify when the meeting ended.

● Clarify the time, date and venue for the next meeting.

Attending the meeting

Hopefully, everybody attending the meeting will be clear why they are there and what they are looking to achieve from their attendance.

Quite often an attendee at the meeting has his or her own item on the agenda. In this case when the item is due to be discussed, the attendee has responsibility for clarifying why that particular item is on the agenda and for letting everybody know what it is that needs to be discussed or decided. If appropriate, a review of events so far should be given.

The types of behaviour that should be avoided by attendees at a meeting include:

- Becoming personal towards either the chairperson or somebody else in the meeting.

- Becoming deflected and trying to refocus the meeting on areas that are outside both the group's influence and the agenda itself.

- Withdrawing from the meeting, and not making any effective contribution.

- Trying to dominate the meeting by virtue of having, perhaps, a more powerful personality.

- Arguing over points for the sake of it.

- Seeking to impress the other attendees. In reality, there may be some inevitability of this approach, by some attendees, particularly in the early part of a meeting.

Some further tips and hints

As we have already mentioned, any meeting that is held must add value to the business unit. Some additional points for you to consider are as follows:

a) Ensure that all participants feel that their opinions have been heard.

b) When possible, ensure that any debate or discussion reaches a tangible and realistic conclusion.

c) Ensure all meetings remain focused and do not deviate from the main items on the agenda.

d) Avoid any agenda being *set* by the manager or team leader. All agendas must cover these current concerns or topical issues of other people attending the meeting.

e) Avoid a meeting becoming an information *dump*.

f) Use the opportunity at team meetings to reinforce messages communicated elsewhere and by other means.

g) Ensure that all attendees have the chance to put items on the agenda prior to the meeting.

h) Consider the possibility of rotating the chair and giving different people the opportunity to chair the meeting each time.

i) Regularly review all meetings that are held. Ask for feedback and suggestions as to how meetings could be improved.

j) Circulate minutes, when produced from meetings. They should be freely circulated and thereby help to create a culture of *open* communication.

k) Remember that for a message to get across, it may need to be repeated in different ways. One example of this is to follow up any presentation with the key messages being reinforced at, say, a weekly team meeting.

8

CHANGE MANAGEMENT

Change is inevitable, it is happening all of the time, everywhere, at a faster rate and in every direction that we look. There are times when change will happen to us, and sometimes we will make the choice to make change happen. This means that we will either have the choice to respond to the change or not, and if change is happening to us, then we must adapt, whether we like it or not.

Change in many ways is a very individual experience – it can include the unexpected – and for each of us will mean slightly different things in terms of the way that we cope, learn about the new change, resist the change, and deal with different levels of crisis on the way. All of us, have had to deal with changes in our lives so far, and that means, perhaps without realizing it, we have had to cope with change even at an instinctive level.

8.1   The change curve

If we study the change curve, we can begin to understand the model that shows how people can react to change. It is based upon a model by Elizabeth Kubler Ross who has all the features listed on the curve itself.

This model can be applied to any sort of change, and it is important that we understand that change can relate to positive as well as potentially negative factors that we have faced or may come to face. According to this change curve, whether the change is positive or otherwise, we go through the same process.

Figure 8.1: Change curve

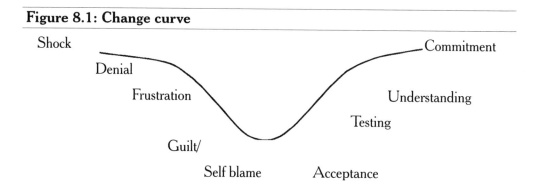

It is important that we understand each of the various stages of the change curve above and we shall consider each one as follows:

Shock

- This is when individuals, faced by the particular change, are in a state of shock, cannot take it all in, and often find themselves in a state of disbelief.

Denial

- This is when an individual may well reject the change, by trying to create the situation in their own mind where they refuse to believe change is happening, or about to happen to them. It is at this stage an individual looks for proof to clarify that this change will never happen (i.e., which is an impossibility), which means that at some stage, usually sooner rather than later, the individual *does* face up to the fact that the change is going to happen. It is at this stage, therefore, that the reality of a change begins to dawn.

Frustration

- At this stage, an individual is still in denial that the change is going to take place. Particularly in the cases where the change is happening to somebody, it is here that an individual feels potentially very frustrated at their inability to be able to influence what is about to happen. Quite often, an individual looks for somebody else to blame for the change that is about to occur.

Guilt/self blame

- A very difficult stage for some individuals in the change curve, because it is here that they really do feel potentially very helpless. At this stage individuals may be looking around, probably seeing others coping or apparently coping more ably with the change, and they themselves may feel quite helpless.

Acceptance

- After a period of time, that will be different for each individual, the period of helplessness, feeling really down about the impending change, starts to draw to a conclusion. Over time, an individual begins, according to this model, to think that things cannot get any worse whatever the change brings. It is at this stage that people begin to consider the new, start to forget the old attitudes or ways of working and actually start to accept that they may not be appropriate any more. It may just be sensible to think about trying to come to terms with the impending changes.

Testing

- This is where individuals begin to *buy in* to the change, and start to feel more positive about it. It may be that individuals try out the new practices, behaviours or whatever else the change implies. It is here that an individual really does start to feel good about the changes.

Understanding

- The rate of acceptance of the change really begins to accelerate here and individuals begin to gain their understanding of changes, accept what this means to them personally, and realize that their full involvement with, and commitment to, the change is inevitable.

Commitment

- This is when an individual has now taken on the change, where the implications of the change have been incorporated into their lives and essentially a part of what they do every day.

This model we have looked at can also be broken down into four main stages as follows:

Denial

This is where people really think change will never happen to them, the impending change will have no affect on them and that whatever it is they are about to face will not be news anyway because they have been around long enough to see it all before. Individuals here often try to ignore any change and just try to carry on with a constant feeling that it will be business as usually indefinitely.

It is at this stage, as a team leader, that there are many things we can begin to do to influence impending change at the outset. These actions include:

- To be aware of any aspects of denial of change in ourselves and those members of our team.

- To try to identify what the problems and issues are for ourselves, if appropriate, and as members in our team.

- To communicate regularly and clearly to our team what the change is about. The communication must have clear and understandable objectives.

- More effective team leaders at this stage clearly understand each member of the team and have a full awareness of how they are feeling at this stage.

- It is also important here for a team leader to be managing this situation in the correct way, dealing with some members of the team on an individual basis, and for some aspects of the change dealing with the team as a whole (i.e., collectively).

- Throughout this potentially challenging stage, the team leader must always appear positive and confident that everything will be alright.

- It is also at this stage that the team leader must be communicating and clarifying the early stages of the particular change.

Resistance

At this second stage of our different way of looking at the change process for an individual it is likely that team members will feel and perhaps be very negative. This will be exhibited in negative body language, individuals acting defensively and perhaps even attempts to undermine the group or to block or refuse to comply with any early stages of the change. The *grapevine* may be a very powerful vehicle at this stage, as those who are attempting to resist the change form a sub-group, with a potentially collective feeling that they really do not have time for the change, it is the team leader's/business's fault that the changes have been made in the first place and that in any case we just do not have time for this.

Again at this stage, the team leader has a very important role to play because, ultimately, it will be the team leader's responsibility to guide the team through this change. The type of things that need to be done include:

- To be fully aware of what is being discussed on the *grapevine* in terms of the change.

- To continue communicating regularly, both on an individual and collective basis. Reinforce messages, be repetitive if necessary.

- Always be seen to be open, honest and reliable (in any case, but particularly at this stage in the change process).

- Be very aware of how the various individuals in your team are behaving at this stage. The potential *saboteurs* need to be identified, and possibly coached in a particular way (in extreme circumstances out of the team!).

- Also, a team leader should identify who is on his or her side and use them to help support this exercise.

Exploration

At this third stage members in the team begin to consider the options available to them with the changes they face. Their mind set will change to begin to ask questions, to be curious about what is happening or about to happen and to feel able to try things out, to take on the possibility that they may need to accept the change.

When this stage is (inevitably?) reached, the team leader can begin to drive the change forward, as this opportunity must be both recognized and grasped. The team leader needs to do the following:

- Try to get each member of the team, now, fully involved in the change.

- Look for ideas from the team both collectively and individually as to how this change process may be taken forward.

- This means the team leader will invite opinion, welcome ideas, and be open to different ways and ideas of how to go forward. Effectively, the team leader is starting to empower the team to generate its own momentum to accept the change.

- Throughout, as with the first two stages, continuous and regular improvement to reinforce the messages and key features of the change is essential.

Commitment

What a change! Whether we use this more simple four-stage approach, or follow the full change curve discussed earlier from start to finish, it is at this *final* stage that we clearly need to avoid being glib and asking what all the fuss was about!

It is at this stage that members of a team take responsibility for the change itself, to begin to make things happen in terms of the new situation. They actively become involved in implementing the change and to develop the new practices and look for ideas for continuous improvement to make the new approach even better.

While in no way adopting a *I told you so* attitude, the team leader again has a pivotal role to play at this stage.

Actions and behaviours of a team leader here include:

- A recognition of the success of the team's incorporating the change into their activities.

- As appropriate, to recognize individuals for their contribution to making the change happen, and to reward and praise team members accordingly.

- Even at this stage, the team leader should still be monitoring progress, recognizing individual contribution and still encouraging this positive approach.

- There will be time when the team leader starts to evaluate how this change has been incorporated into work activities, and to see what lessons can be learnt as a group and on an individual basis.

This (simpler) change process can be illustrated as below:

Figure 8.2: Four-stage change

Denial	Commitment
Resistance	Exploration

We have looked at two theoretical models of how the change process can evolve. You will, of course, immediately realize that it is never as simple as this because changes these days are continuous, and we are not in the situation that we only have to cope with one change at a time. For each of us, we are coping with having to adapt to many changes on a daily basis not only in our working lives, but outside as well. This therefore makes any process discussed above one that must be multi-dimensional. Of all the changes that we face, and that our team members face, will be at different stages, at different times and for different reasons. It may also be the case that depending on which specific change we are talking about, an individual will be coping with that in the most positive or otherwise way, which then means that the various stages on the change curve will be for longer or shorter periods of time. What we really do need to understand is that the change process is one that is actually quite complex although without doubt inevitable.

8.2   Managing people through change

We have looked at some of the theoretical dimensions of the change process and some of the actions and behaviour of individuals within a team and that a team leader may be expected to exhibit.

We also need to remember how we might be feeling, or how our team members may be feeling, during a change.

Leaving behind the *old way* may well be leaving members of our team, and possibly ourselves, with a feeling of loss and sadness. It may well be that something we have been doing for a long period of time, possibly many many years, will become a thing of the past, and as a result our own work existence in the way that we have been used to may be being undermined. Understandably, individuals may well feel undervalued and that their own personal abilities are under scrutiny and threat.

As the change process that we have looked at evolves, there will come a stage when individuals feel a range of emotions. From one extreme of isolation and being in the wilderness to the other an urgent desire to understand and test out the new ways of working. Also at this time, all individuals begin, all at different periods of time, to accept that their old ways are no longer applicable and that change is coming their way.

As the new world approaches there will be feelings of various degrees of anticipation, inevitably entwined with apprehension. As the new way dawns feelings will be one of old habits as history combined with high expectations of what is to come. Relative energy levels, individually and collectively, will begin to rise as a sense of excitement and anticipation begin to build.

Resistance to change and why change may fail

Quite often, people will be comfortable with the way things are, and on this basis there will be no recognition of the need to change. Even if a group has battled on in a poor situation for some time, should any change imply a major disruption to the way they do things, it may be that initially they would prefer to stay as they are. In any case, change can be quite painful insofar as it can be radical and cause upset, dissatisfaction and great resistance from individuals within a team.

On all occasions, even if the current scenario is one that is intolerable and obviously not working as well as it might, a group of people will not move forward in the change process unless there is some agreed understanding about where it is they are trying to get to. The group will not move forward collectively until *each* individual within that group does become fully aware as to what the objectives of the change are and where exactly it is they are trying to move to.

As a team leader it dangerous to assume that dissatisfaction will always be the first response to news of any impending change. It may not always be the case. In addition, as a team leader you will be expected to *drive* (albeit carefully!) your team through change – it is absolutely critical that throughout you are aware what each of your individual team members is going through on a personal level. This means each member of your team must be treated slightly differently, handled in a different way and motivated to change on a very personal level. Whatever happens, with us as members, each of our team members must be motivated to accept the change and to see it as a move for the better.

Why change fails

Examples when major change management has been critical in the past few years include when total quality management has been introduced to an organization, with business process re-engineering, or when an organization has restructured.

In many cases, the underlying reason for any proposed change are marketplace driven. These *drivers* include:

The evolution towards a global marketplace, prevailing and future economic conditions; the increasing influence of technology; changes in the competitive situation in a particular marketplace.

We have been considering earlier some of the ways in which change can work and we need now to review some of the reasons why a change initiative may not be successful.

Some of the reasons for this include:

1) Where throughout, there is a fundamental misunderstanding as to what the change actually is. We have considered earlier that change is not implemented as a result of a half-day workshop, or after a management briefing. It is potentially a long and very complex process which will not be implemented successfully as a result of a *one-off* event.

2) Due to the complexity of the whole process, it is essential that an appropriate amount of planning and preparation takes place beforehand. A successful change initiative will be a large part the result of very careful preparation and planning.

3) Throughout the whole process of change it is crucial that everybody involved knows

exactly where it is they are trying to get to. Therefore, the lack of adequate communication and availability of information will always be an impediment to change.

4) In our working lives, all of us are touching and feeling change every day. The rate of change is accelerating and will continue to accelerate. In this sense change is infinite, and is ongoing. One could argue that change is a long-term process, and must be managed as such. Nevertheless, the whole process must be *broken down* to smaller segments, so that team leaders and team members can actually see and feel that they are making progress, possibly in shorter-term steps.

5) We have already seen how complex the change process is. This means that a successful change initiative is not usually be achieved by merely organizing workshops, providing posters and circulars and the accompanying communication to go with these.

6) Communication is crucial, it is an essential part of *BAU* management activity, and arguably it is even more critical during times of change (which again you could argue is *BAU*). The communication process should be well planned and structured, very frequent, and carried out on a collective and individual basis. You need to make sure that the *grapevine* is working with you during a time of change, and not against you.

7) Change is inevitable, and for many organizations there is a clear need to change in order to survive. In some cases this means change must be something that is possible, necessary and achievable. This approach can be hindered by any historical experiences within an organization where change has been badly managed.

8) There have been examples over recent years where a proposed change has failed because of employee resistance. The definition of failure is one of degree. At the extreme a change process could be called to a halt, or, more likely, not be as successful as it could have been where part of a team or workforce does not commit fully to the particular change.

9) A successful change initiative means that the whole team needs to be prepared to go through what is to come. As well as many of the dimensions we have discussed previously, all appropriate members of the team need to have the necessary training to help them cope with and adapt to the future change. This training may well be about the change itself, and it could be knowledge or skills based, providing new skills in readiness for the change or consolidating existing knowledge and ability.

9

DEVELOPMENT

9.1 Planning your personal development

Essentially, any individual will develop if he or she is able to focus on his or her own development. More often than not people are less responsive to ideas for their own development imposed from above, or even relating to their recent appraisals. Personal development must be about a member of staff focusing on his or her own development needs and evolving these needs into a specific plan of action, which should result in those ideas leading to self-development.

Understanding a development need

In its simplest format a development need can be one of the following:

- An area of skill you need to develop.

- An area of technical ability that you need to improve upon.

- To be smarter about the way you go about things (behaviour).

- Developing a particular competency.

- Improving a level of knowledge in a certain area.

These developmental areas can then be used to either improve people's performance in their current job, or to focus on areas that are likely to be needed for a job which they are aiming for in the future.

To gain maximum value from assessing development needs you need to be as specific as possible, and areas to consider are as follows:

- To be aware of the specific requirements of your current job.

- To be aware of specific requirements in your current job that are perhaps not being fulfilled to the required standards or alternatively are particular strengths which could be done even better.

- To be clear about plans for future development and career progression (as realistically as possible in today's ever-changing job climate).

● Assuming the organization supports a culture of self-development, to consider how that development will improve business performance.

The benefits of personal development

Clearly the working world is becoming ever more competitive and organizations remorselessly demand and expect increased levels of performance from their employees. This situation is reflected in appraisal processes with various job targets becoming more stretching every year. Cultures of *continuous improvement* are becoming more prevalent.

It therefore follows that it is to the benefit of employees to consider how they may be able to do their job more effectively and thereby increase their contribution to the business. Not only should this lead to more individual recognition from local management but also, if focused in the appropriate way, help to facilitate any future career development.

A plan of action

It is very easy to talk about what you intend to do; to change your thoughts to action can often be facilitated by committing your plan to paper and constantly referring to it, or making it permanently visible by displaying it on the office wall.

If this approach is adopted, clearly a developed plan can be flexible to suit individual needs. A plan could cover a year, a few months or even a few weeks for a specific developmental need. Care needs to be taken that a plan is realistic, and not overambitious. Perhaps a discussion with line management or colleagues will help to clarify which areas of an individual's development should be concentrated upon first of all. However long the initial development plan is scheduled for, it should be constantly reviewed and up-dated.

In any case, the journey of personal development is infinite, it is a constant process of review and adapting to change in circumstances, job conditions, varying business objectives and changing career aspirations.

One key point in all of this is that ownership of any development plan must rest with the individual concerned. There is no doubt that unless an individual is aware of his or her own development needs, he or she will not give a total commitment to taking any remedial or developmental action.

The role of the manager in an individual's development

In today's working world the ownership for personal development rests with the individual. In the vast majority of cases, the responsibility for learning new skills, or preparing for the *next job*, or making oneself more marketable, rests with the individual employee. It is therefore very unlikely that a personal development plan will be imposed on an individual by line management.

The manager does have a critical role both by creating the work environment where self-development is encouraged and welcomed, and by being approachable by individual members of staff to chat through any ideas they have for their own self development. In some cases regular reviews, mentioned above, are undertaken by line management; alternatively, of course, other colleagues may become involved.

Discussing personal development with line management can also be useful, because the reality of the plan can be considered. Your manager (and colleagues) will have a view as to how sensible and realistic a plan of action is – *best practice* would then indicate management facilitating as much help and support that is required to complete the plan.

Other key roles a manager may take include:

- Providing leadership and vision.

- Motivating individuals by recognizing and reinforcing effective performance.

- Coaching and developing individuals.

- Establishing appropriate business goals and performance standards – explaining what needs to be accomplished and why.

- Providing employees with all the information they need to do their job well and to form a partnership with the organization.

- Involving employees in decisions affecting them.

- Leading by example.

- Encouraging individuals to be innovative.

- Delegating responsibility to individuals, both appropriate to their current abilities and relative to their identified development needs.

Ultimately, however, it is an individual's responsibility to make that plan a reality.

Figure 9.1

Development needs	Action to be taken	Date	Review date	Individual benefits

Above there is an example of what a development plan could look like. It is very simple and easy to complete, deliberately so, and it should therefore facilitate individual development rather than hinder it by becoming a bureaucratic exercise.

As we have already mentioned, when filling in the column *developmental needs*, there is a need to be as specific as possible.

Potential *actions* to be taken include the following:

- Attending an internal or external training course.

- Reading books or articles.

- Completing a specific project to provide the necessary specific development experience.

- Discussing various developmental aspects with your manager or colleagues.

- Attending college or evening classes, for example.

As we have mentioned in the preceding paragraphs, individual development is just that, an individually driven exercise. It can remain that way, or perhaps a more desirable approach is to discuss ongoing progress with line management and colleagues – an individual may receive further feedback by adopting this approach, which may in turn confirm other areas for future development, and in addition other areas for development may evolve.

9.2   Individual self-development

When people are looking to the future in terms of their career they will often ask some of the following questions:

- What opportunities are there for me to develop within my existing role?

- Should I be looking for a different role?

- If I am looking for a different role, where should I be looking?

It will make good sense for anybody considering to follow up these questions to already have thought about the answers.

A major part in making these types of decisions is an honest and clear understanding about what motivates you personally and to be very aware of what it is that is important to you. Ultimately, the values that an individual holds are just that, and the values which an individual actually has are not those values which they feel they ought to have. Ultimately, a decision taken on an individual's self-development because they are based on somebody else's values will lead to regret, and some level of dissatisfaction.

There are many areas to consider when deciding which way your career should go, and some of these will be work-related and others be based around factors outside of the workplace. Some of these key criteria include:

- How important your career objectives are to you.

- How much you enjoy accepting new challenges and facing new experiences.

- How competitive you are by nature and how much you want to be *the best*.

- How important money is to you.

- Where your family fits in to the overall equation.

● Would you naturally strive to continuously develop yourself?

● Exactly what is your own ideal balance between achieving your work and domestic objectives?

These various aspects are complex in themselves, but also need to be imposed on the ever-changing world of work. Years ago those who wanted to develop their career may have expected to have a new job every two or three years within one organization. The culture may well have been if you did not achieve this then somehow there was something wrong. In some ways there was a self-fulfilling promotion culture. In today's world in most organizations this kind of career growth is not sustainable and for some this becomes a cause of major concern. An alternative view is that an individual career is about fulfilling the things that are important to you personally rather than focusing only on achieving regular promotions.

In today's world, nothing in life, no job, no activity is guaranteed to satisfy an individual's (ever-changing) values all of the time. This is why an individual needs to be very aware about what is important to him or her.

By reflecting back on some of the major decisions you have made in life, both good or otherwise, you may become more aware about the *actual* values that you (and your family) hold. This exercise will enable you to learn a little more about yourself, perhaps. It may also help you to begin to *design* a framework for taking important decisions. You may also be surprised because by reflecting back in this way you may learn that you (and your family) have some values that were not actually evident at that time.

Overall then let us be clear about what we are trying to do in terms of an individual's self-development:

a) For each individual to establish a series of values that will provide a framework to take good career decisions.

b) To be clear about the values that you (and your family) hold and give a clear focus on what you want to achieve.

c) To clarify the values you hold, which will help you to get the maximum personal satisfaction from your the current job.

Conducting your own self-audit

All of us from time to time need to review where we are now and why, and where we are trying to get to, and for what reason. It therefore makes sense to undergo regular self appraisal or reviews to help us to make some new-formed assessments. Ways in which this can be done include:

● An individual self-assessment of your own strengths and development needs. Clearly this assessment must be done realistically and honestly.

● Be fully aware of the key responsibilities that you have, and how effectively you are able to meet and exceed these responsibilities.

- Proactively seek feedback and opinion on your own self-assessment from those whose opinions you respect. These may include management, peers, subordinates or family.

- Look back on any previous reports or annual appraisals which will generate data and ideas from your strengths and development needs.

When looking forward, you should be very clear about what sort of job you are looking to strive for. In that context this self-appraisal will help you to understand what experience, competencies and potential you have to make you a prime contender for that job. Concurrently, you should become more self-aware of what developmental areas you have to try to rectify prior to your becoming a realistic contender for the job you are aiming for. In today's working world of rapid change, by implication it may be a little naive to focus all your efforts on achieving one particular job. This job may go or may change due to circumstances which you cannot see today but may well be with us by tonight or tomorrow.

Without doubt, the primary responsibility for an individual's development and job satisfaction rests with that individual.

An individual in a radically changing job marketplace

There have been huge demographic changes in the last century, and now the world spends much more money on communications and technology than it does on farming, industry, mining and construction. As we project towards the future, the workforces around the world will change as follows:

- More and more people will become self-employed.

- Many individuals will be working from home.

- The *cradle to the grave* employer/employee relationship will have ended. Many full-time people will be employed on short-term contracts.

- More people will be working part-time.

- It will be much more important to make yourself not only geographically mobile but also marketable across the job market(s) which you personally target for your own employment aspirations.

- All of us will be living in an ever-increasingly uncertain world where it is essential that we keep learning and remember that it is our own responsibility to develop our own individual careers.

Things you can do to facilitate your own development

Undertake a personal development plan

A personal development plan is a plan that will help you to plan your own development. Usually it is not a plan that is imposed by management or necessarily based upon appraisals. It is a plan that will help you to focus your own ideas about the future and how you can link plans for your own development to these ideas. As a result, a personal development plan can record activities that may help you to improve your job performance in your current role, or help to prepare you for an application some time in the future for a new role.

In a personal development plan a development need, or needs are the basis of this plan. A development need is usually one of the following:

- An area of skill, technical ability or a particular behaviour, or perhaps even an area of knowledge that you need to develop or improve upon in your current role.

- A skill, competency, behaviour or area of knowledge that you personally feel you would like to acquire or develop in order to improve your chances of progressing, at some point in the future, to a different job.

A personal development plan will enable you to keep a record which can then be regularly reviewed. It will therefore be much easier for you to be able to look back over recent months to assess where you have improved.

A personal development plan, then, may cover any particular period of time that is appropriate to you. This may be for a year, or for a period of a few weeks. Whatever the period of time, the plan must be dynamic, which means it must be constantly reviewed and up-dated.

Remember the ownership of this plan rests with you, the individual, although ideally line management will play an active role in supporting you.

This managerial support will include discussing the contents of the plan with the individual, agreeing to meet regularly to review progress, confirming any priorities within the plan and to being available for advice and guidance.

The type of options that may be included on a development plan include:

- Undertaking research for wider reading.

- Being involved in a project or special assignment as a platform to provide the developmental experience.

- Being seconded to a different place of work.

A *model* personal development plan could look as follows:

Individual development need	(Agreed) Course of action	Target date	Comments/key points
1)			
2)			
3)			

You will see that the above table focuses on three areas. It is very important not to be overambitious, and in reality if an individual focuses on three or maybe four developmental areas at any one it should be something that is achievable.

Selling yourself

There are many ways in which you may have the opportunity to do this; it may be in a face-to-face environment or in writing.

In terms of career development, the opportunities to sell yourself in writing may well be through a job application form or a CV. Obviously, when selling yourself in writing, your primary objective is to differentiate yourself from everybody else. This means your CV should:

● Be concise.

● Probably be on no more than two sides of A4 paper.

● Ensure that the *employment* aspect of your CV runs in reverse chronological order, commencing with your present job and working backwards.

● Try to demonstrate how you have used the competencies needed for the job for which you are applying.

If you are preparing for an interview, for some of you it may well be the first time you have had an interview since the day you joined the organization. Remember that interview processes have changed dramatically, and will continue to change as they become more professionally conducted and challenging.

Prior to an interview you need to prepare thoroughly. You may be faced with more than one interviewer with either one or both interviewers asking questions, or perhaps one person interviewing and the other person taking notes. Part of the interview process may be to challenge you on what you have already discussed in your CV by giving you the opportunity to use your own work experiences to illustrate your experiences. At the interview stage you will also have the opportunity to ask questions, and this is your opportunity to show the interviewer how much you have thought about the role for which you are applying, and to demonstrate how much you want that job.

After each interview you attend, if you can, it is important to get feedback on your performance. This means getting feedback on both your interview performance and also how well your job application, in writing, was received.

Overall

A theme throughout this section is that we must acknowledge that your career progression *must* be based upon satisfying your own honest and individual values. Any individual ambitions for the future must be achieved in an environment of rapid, radical and continual change. Those who progress the most will be those who can live in and adapt to this constantly changing environment. One key success criterion will be the ability to continually learn and develop and to have an ongoing thirst for acquiring new knowledge and skills. Within this, each of us needs to be realistic about our own aspirations while remembering the responsibility for our own individual development remains and will always remain with each of us alone.

9.3   Investors in People

The Investors in People standard (IIP) recognizes *best practice* in the management, training and development of its people and its organization through:

- Developing the potential of all employees.

- Commitment to training and development for all of its employees to help to achieve business goals.

- Regularly reviewing the training and development needs of all employees.

- Taking action to train and develop individuals throughout their time of employment with an organization.

- Assessing its investment in training and development to ensure success in an environment of continuous improvement.

In this context everybody within an organization, by a commitment to their own role and by taking responsibility for their own development, is involved in this IIP process. Also, management, team leaders and supervisors have responsibilities to coach, counsel, train, appraise and provide ongoing feedback to their teams.

To gain IIP accreditation the following activities need to be taking place:

Commitment

This means an IIP organization has made a statement and commitment right from the very top to develop all of its employees to help to meet business objectives.

This commitment from the top needs to be effectively communicated throughout the organization. At each level employees need to be aware of the broad aims of the organization and how they personally may make an effective contribution to its overall success.

Reviewing

This is where an organization is aware of the training needs and developmental requirements of each member of staff and regularly reviews and adapts these plans accordingly.

A written although adaptable training plan should be in place and this plan will identify ongoing training needs together with actions to be taken to meet these training needs. Ongoing business requirement circumstances will be changing, and accordingly ongoing training needs and requirements need to be regularly reviewed and plans amended (at an organizational and individual level).

It also needs to be clear that an organization is aware of the resource implications of providing this training and that it is known and visible who has the responsibility for ensuring this training takes place throughout the organization. The IIP process also looks for evidence of objectives being set for training and development actions throughout the organization and particularly at an individual level. It may be that some of these objectives are linked to relevant qualifications, or external standards (for example, National Vocational Qualifications – NVQs).

Action

This is where an organization is seen to be active in training and developing all of their employees throughout the period of time that an employee is working for it.

This process begins with an effective induction process whereby a person new to the organization is given all the appropriate training and development they need to begin the new job.

On a more local level managers are seen to be active in carrying out their responsibilities for training and developing their team members and being supportive and fully involved in doing this. At the same time a working environment should be created where individual members of staff are encouraged to identify their own training and developmental needs, and be aware of what training and development opportunities are available to them. A partnership is then created between management and staff whereby a training and development plan can be agreed to help to meet individual training and developmental needs.

Evaluation

Evaluation is where an organization that is investing in training and developing its people is aware how effective this investment is and what affect this training and development is having upon the progress of the organization.

Generally, this evaluation focuses upon the impact that training and development has on overall levels of knowledge, skills and attitude. Evaluation will reach some conclusions of how training and development is impacted on the effectiveness of an organization in terms of meeting its business objectives. Top management and managers need to be aware of the costs of training and development, and the resulting benefits this training and development is having (i.e., a broad cost-benefit appraisal).

On an ongoing basis, there needs to be clear evidence that any conclusions drawn from the evaluation process are being seen to be acted upon as a part of management's ongoing commitment to the training and development process.

The IIP assessment

There are two elements to the IIP assessment: firstly, the portfolio of evidence and secondly the interviews. These are weighted 20% – 80% respectively. This means having the requisite processes and policies in place to meet the standards accounts for only 20% of the final assessment, whereas 80% relates to how an organization makes them work and what people actually experience as a result. To pass the IIP assessment a 70% minimum score is required.

Portfolio of evidence

The purpose of a portfolio is to document the processes and practices relating to people's development within an organization and to give the IIP assessors an overall picture. Assessors need this information to help to understand the culture of an organization and to be clear about how an organization has evolved over recent years, recent changes it has undergone and will undertake, and to have some understanding of present and future priorities. This process begins to give the assessors a clearer picture of who it is they wish to speak to at the interview stage.

All different parts of an organization contribute to the overall portfolio of evidence, and the assessors look to see how different parts of the organization integrate with each other in terms of the overall training and development strategy. Various parts of an organization are asked to provide some *evidence or audit trails* which provide details of how particular training and development initiatives developed from the outset through to the evaluation stage. Usually, at this research stage and when the assessors are looking at particular training and development initiatives, they start to make requests about who they would wish to interview.

Either individuals are selected specifically, or the assessors request to speak to a range of people from different parts of the business. Undoubtedly the assessors will look to speak a mix of men and women at all levels throughout an organization, and with varying ranges of service, and include a number of key-time staff.

The interviews

These interviews take place on a one-to-one basis and their primary purpose is to draw conclusions about whether the IIP standards have been met in relation to the various activities undertaken by any unit within an organization. In fact, the IIP assessors may see the portfolio as being impressive, although this will be no guarantee that in practice the employees are experiencing the benefits of IIP. The assessors are looking to see an organization and the individuals working in it working together and conscientiously using the four principals identified earlier, often on a *best practice* basis and incorporating the short- and long-term plans and aims.

At an interview with an IIP assessor, the individual is not expected to explain the whole IIP philosophy or be familiar with each of the (currently 23) IIP indicators. Typically, these interviews are carried out in a relaxed way, with the IIP assessor trying to draw out facts from an individual using a series of probing questions. By using this type of questioning technique an assessor is able to *mark* a business unit against many of the 23 indicators.

The IIP assessors are experienced enough to understand what an interviewee is saying and, for example, to be able to see through any negative attitudes. Their questioning technique is partly designed to clarify whether a particular process or practice mentioned in the portfolio does actually occur and work in practice. The assessors are looking for elements of consistency across an organization in the responses they get, when determining success (or otherwise) against the key indicators. It is important to understand that the IIP assessors are not there to dictate what systems should be in place, for example, the use of a particular appraisal system. Instead, as we have seen above, the assessors read about and try to understand the culture of an organization, together with its key objectives. On this basis, through the ongoing understanding of the portfolio, and with the interview process, they are able to judge whether the systems that are in place actually work well for that particular organization. Furthermore, apart from simply seeing evidence of what happens the assessors require written evidence of how these various systems work in practice – for example, how managers demonstrate their commitment to the training and development of their staff.

Another vital area of the assessment is the principle of evaluation, because IIP experience to date shows that this tends to be the weakest area. Assessors pay particular attention to how any investment in training and development is measured at the highest levels in an organization. In addition, the assessors expect to see clear measures in place to evaluate training and development at every level of an organization.

When an IIP assessment is taking place, each individual has the possibility of being chosen for an interview, which means that every individual in an organization has a key part to play in achieving the IIP standard. If asked, it is essential that each individual can demonstrate active understanding and involvement in each of the four categories of the IIP philosophy.

9.4   Manpower planning

Manpower planning can be defined as "a strategy for the acquisition, utilization, improvement and retention of an organization's human resources".

There are several guiding principles for manpower planning, as follows:

● Manpower planning must be seen as an integral part of the corporate planning process. This means that those senior management who are involved in manpower planning need to be aware how their actions fit in with the overall needs and requirements of the business.

- The manpower plan needs to be sponsored by top management.

- Particularly in larger organizations, manpower planning should be coordinated from one central point. This means that the overall process is managed in a focused and centralized way.

- Manpower planning can work to its maximum effect only if all personnel records are kept up to date.

- Any manpower plan needs to be long enough to add value but not too long (which could mean that circumstances may have changed to make the manpower plan meaningless). Typically, this means that the plan is for one to two year's duration.

- The way in which the manpower plan is put together needs to be constantly reviewed as prevailing circumstances inevitably change, and over time an organization also gains greater experience in working with a manpower plan.

Within the guiding principles given above, there are several other aspects of manpower planning that we need to consider.

The investigation stage

This is where research is undertaken so that an overall understanding of the organization is gained and the basis on which the manpower plan is drawn up is established. Those producing the plan need clearly to understand the environment in which the organization operates, what challenges the organization is facing and how well its current people resource is being used. At this stage also, it needs to be established how the people requirements of the organization are being met:

- Where are the skills gaps?

- Are various parts of the organization working in harmony to develop people across the organization?

- What role (and how effectively) does the human resources department play?

Forecasting the future

This aspect of the manpower plan is concerned with projecting into the future in terms of which way the organization is heading. This is important because the manpower plan is looking to provide maximum return to the organization from its people resource. Maximum return will be achieved only if an organization's people resource are *adding value* to the organization with optimum effect. The manpower planners need to be aware of what is likely to happen in the future so that future demands for people can be established, and that plans can begin to be made to equate this demand with what supply is available either internally from the organization or externally from the marketplace.

Planning

This stage of the manpower planning process is where the demand for particular types of people is matched with the likely supply of those people over the period of the manpower plan. The likely features of this stage in the manpower planning process include:

- The recruitment process.

- The associated aspects of training and development – this is, where existing employees are re-trained as appropriate, and any newcomers to the organization receive the appropriate training in the particular skills areas.

- The pay and reward structure – which is designed to attract recruits into the organization and motivate those who are already working for it.

- The need for harmonious industrial relations – throughout the manpower planning process, it is highly desirable that existing employees positively support the manpower plan, and that productive relationships are maintained with any representative organizations.

- The need to accommodate any known changes over the planning period.

The demand and supply equation

Basically there are two sides to manpower planning, demand and supply, and we shall now consider each aspect in turn.

Demand

Establishing the demand means forecasting the likely demands the organization will have for people at all levels in the future.

Aspects of the demands side of the equation include:

- A number of people that need to complete particular tasks (job analysis is helpful here).

- How many people are needed to complete various tasks – previous records can be helpful, but in many organizations requirements are changing due to the impact of technology. In some larger organizations, regular work studies take place where many jobs are *measured*.

- What are the various skill levels currently within the organization, as against the skill levels that are required now and in the future?

- To meet the required levels of demand, what will be the associated costs?

Supply

The supply side of the equation considers the availability in terms of quality and quantity of manpower that is available (now and in the future) from inside and outside the organization. Aspects of the supply equation include staff turnover, current and likely future movements within the organization (promotions, transfers), recruitment and retention rates, and the conditions in the workplace (now and in the future).

Some areas to consider at this stage include:

- Researching each of the organization's employees to ensure that their personnel records are kept up to date (showing details of their current role, skills and qualifications).

- For each employee, effectively an audit should be undertaken to detail their potential for undertaking different jobs in the future, perhaps on a level move basis, or for promotion.

- Consideration should be given as to how an organization's people can be used with most effect (i.e., to add the most value) during the period of manpower plan.

In reality, most organizations seek maximum advantage in using the employees they already have. Significant re-training may be required to accommodate the future needs of the organization and there many be significant cost implications. Some organizations consider what gap in the manpower plan can be filled by external recruitment and take the decision to import particular skills from outside.

The supply equation has an internal dimension which we have considered above and an external aspect, which may have some of the following features:

- The availability of particular skills in the local economy.

- Levels of employment locally and regionally.

- Competition from other organizations. Potential new entrants into the organization with similar skills and abilities.

- Where the organization is located (in terms of being in a place that will attract people to want to come and live and work).

- Common policy – for example, in equal opportunities, sex discrimination, age discrimination and disability.

- Local and national patterns, now and in the future, for education and training.

- The trend towards part-time working.

During the course of the manpower plan, primarily the human resource department will have responsibility for achieving a balance between the demand and supply of the equation. Once this reconciliation has been achieved on an ongoing basis, the effectiveness of the recruitment process, the training and development support, the harmony of industrial relations, the rewards and recognition systems, will all be seen. Each of these dimensions is a complex area in itself, and all have to be managed in an effective way to play their part in the overall equation.

In reality, no manpower plan can be *cast in stone*. As with any plan, flexibility is crucial and all manpower plans, and the various aspects within them, have to be regularly reviewed, possibly as a result of changes in the overall organizational objectives or corporate plan, or due to changes in technology or possible merger activity, for example.

Succession planning

There are some critical aspects of succession planning that should be considered, as follow:

- We have already seen that the manpower plan determines what people requirements will be needed over a forecast period of between, say, two and ten years.

- A succession plan is made on the basis of projecting into the future all of the requirements of the various parts of an organization. It anticipates changes in the required management, people experience and qualifications, and what departments or business units within an organization are likely to change, grow, disappear or amalgamate. Crucial to this aspect of the succession plan is up-to-date records being kept on all members of staff because succession planners must have access to details on individual's age, qualifications, experience and future potential.

- In a succession plan there are elements of priority, usually under three broad headings:

  - *Immediate term* Usually for short-term periods only.

  - *Medium term* Say for one to five years in the future.

  - *Longer term* For a five to ten year period in the future.

  In reality any immediate successors will be those who are easily accessible and possibly already within the organization. They may already be acting as a deputy or have perhaps covered for an individual during time of absence or holiday, for example.

  Succession planning for the middle term gives an organization more options, because they can look from inside the organization or department or possibly outside.

  Looking towards the long term means that further changes will inevitably need to be anticipated and reacted to. The longer-term aspects will also enable any members of an organization on a *fast track* career path to be accommodated, as well as looking at the broader requirements of an organization's people requirements over a longer period of time.

- Succession plans provide a systematic approach not only for moving people around in an organization, for promotion and inter-business unit transfer, but also for considering how to cater for those who leave the organization (perhaps due to retirement). A succession plan enables the specifics of the training and development required for the successors to be planned for and to accommodate, for example, job rotation as part of that process.

- Of course, the succession plan is a plan, and it has a crucial human dimension. Clearly, this plan must be more than a paper exercise – those that are involved in any projected moves in the future must clearly have some *buy in* to the process. Ideally, the moves projected in the succession plan will meet the expectations of the individuals concerned, but quite often it is not always this straightforward. In the extreme some managers are so disappointed with their futures as given in the succession plan they exit the organization. An organization must try to achieve an appropriate balance between how much of the succession planning should be shared with those involved, and at what stage. There is no ideal solution, and much will depend on existing practices within the organization and the expectations of the people themselves. In some cases, it is accepted that succession planning is a strictly confidential activity and very few, if any, will be advised beforehand of what is planned for them.

10

SELF MANAGEMENT

10.1   Time management

Time marches on, an indisputable fact which means that time that has passed will not and cannot be recovered. All of us therefore have a period of time at our disposal which we must endeavour to use as effectively as possible.

For each of us, if we were to analyse our performance and activities both inside and outside of work, and consider how effectively we use that time, there will be ways in which we can get a greater return on how we achieve both our business and personal goals.

Ways in which we can do this include:

- Analysing one's own job performance.

- Obtaining feedback and guidance from others.

- Devise a plan of action to project how your behaviour will change as you use your time more effectively.

Some issues to consider

All of us can benefit from taking the time to consider what we are looking to achieve in all aspects of our life in the short- and slightly longer-term. Clearly, however, circumstances change as do priorities, which means these *projections* need to be regularly used, reviewed and possibly re-prioritized.

In filling out the charts on the following pages it will be useful to be as specific as possible, focusing on what you actually want to achieve at work and at home, rather than what you would think about doing. It is also important to be ambitious, while being realistic, thinking about the constraints that you face in reality.

Figure 10.1: Aims, ambitions, achievements – 12 months

Domestic	Work/Career
Relationships	Others

Figure 10.2: Aims, ambitions, achievements – 5-year plan

Domestic	Work/Career
Relationships	Others

It may be that you wish to project farther forward, say, for 10 years. You are the best judge of this, although in any work context where there is an environment of rapid change you may need to review this particular chart very regularly!

When this exercise has been done, the outcome – providing you have been very honest with yourself – will give you some main aims and objectives to achieve over the next few years. This means the way you use your time needs to be prioritized accordingly.

Understanding why our time goes so quickly in the workplace!

All of us can empathize with those days when we find it is time to go home and we have not achieved what we set out to do. Sometimes there can be very good reasons for this – an immediate crisis, a colleague being away from the office, among other reasons.

There is one way, again focusing on the themes of being honest and ruthless with the way that we record what we do, we can analyse what we do in our day-to-day work activities. The process is really quite simple, because all we need to do is to break down in detail what you do on a day-by-day basis.

A suggested way to proceed is as follows:

- Record and detail all activities that take, say, more than 10 minutes (or any other figure that is felt to be realistic).

- Record details of all your *time stealers* or interruptions.

- Focus on what *actually* happens rather than what you think is happening.

- If your job is cyclical, over a day, a week or even a month, ensure that you record your activities for an appropriate period of time so that sensible conclusions can be drawn.

- When you look at the amount of time that is spent doing priority activities, these in turn should have some order of priority. It may be that you are very clear about what your priority activities should be, and in what order they need to be completed – if this is not the case then an early discussion with line management would seem appropriate.

It is sensible to record your findings on paper, perhaps as follows:

Day	Time	Details of Activity/Time Stealer/Events/Interruptions
Monday	9.00 am	
	10.00 am	
	11.00 am	
	12.00 pm	
	1.00 pm	
	2.00 pm	
	3.00 pm	
	4.00 pm	
	5.00 pm	
Tuesday	9.00 am	
	10.00 am	
	11.00 am	
	12.00 pm	
	1.00 pm	
	2.00 pm	

	3.00 pm	
	4.00 pm	
	5.00 pm	
Wednesday	9.00 am	
	10.00 am	
	11.00 am	
	12.00 pm	
	1.00 pm	
	2.00 pm	
	3.00 pm	
	4.00 pm	
	5.00 pm	
Thursday	9.00 am	
	10.00 am	
	11.00 am	
	12.00 pm	
	1.00 pm	
	2.00 pm	
	3.00 pm	
	4.00 pm	
	5.00 pm	
Friday	9.00 am	
	10.00 am	
	11.00 am	
	12.00 pm	
	1.00 pm	
	2.00 pm	
	3.00 pm	
	4.00 pm	
	5.00 pm	

Please note, the 9.00 am – 5.00 pm timespan is merely an example – these days there are many options on people's working hours, whether it be a continental shift system, part-time, full-time or even working many more hours (voluntarily or otherwise!) than anticipated.

Once you have completed your self audit, then you need to make effective use of this information.

Possible suggestions are:

● In your earlier activity when you looked at work/career ambitions for the short-term and longer-term, consider how you are actually spending your time and how it fits in with these plans.

● Review rigourously your findings in your self-audit and consider (perhaps discuss with your line manager) about how much of these activities are actually yours. Are they activities that fit in with your job responsibilities and accountabilities, or should the activities be done elsewhere?

● Like the vast majority of people, when you total up the amount of time that you actually spend focusing on the priority areas of your job, compared to the *time stealers* or interruptions, you can quickly see there are possible (or definite!) areas for action.

Suggested ways to improve your own time management

The areas that follow are suggestions to help. The number of suggestions is not exhaustive and not intended to be specific to every job – there will be a need to adapt and apply some of the points to your own job.

1) Consider your job priorities. Everybody should be specifically aware about each of the tasks he or she needs to do, and how important each task is in terms of priority and urgency.

A practical way of making progress here is to visualize your activities on a grid similar to the one below.

Figure 10.3

Urgent – Important Top Priority	Important – Non-urgent Second Priority
Not important – Urgent Third Priority	Not important – non-urgent I am not sure you should be doing this!

The definitions of urgent and important may well have to be agreed locally between yourself and your line manager, although the suggestions are as follows:

Important – an activity that will impact in a significant way on an individual meeting their personal job objectives.

Urgent – an activity that needs to be done to meet a deadline.

When the above grid has been completed most of us find that we put various items in each of the boxes. Again if this is done in an honest and open way, most of us will find some areas which we could immediately think about adjusting, thereby giving us an opportunity to use our time more effectively.

It is also likely that items in the first three priority boxes then need to be prioritized in each box, so that for example in the top priority box, where activities are both urgent and important, they themselves have to be prioritized.

2) Use a *"to do"* list – this is a widely used activity across many organizations, simple to use and if followed rigourously will help each of us to ensure our priorities are met.

Essentially, following on the points above, when various priorities have been categorized according to their urgency, we can then in a very simple format use a *to do list*.

One possible lay-out is as follows:

Activity	*Priority	Time taken

*What needs to be transposed on a *to do list* are clearly identified activities from your *urgent and important* activities and tasks that have then themselves been prioritized. You may wish to annotate the top priorities as 1 or A, and next priorities as 2 or B, for example. As with everything else that we have looked at so far, all these lists need to be *used*, kept up-to-date and *regularly* reviewed.

3) Use of the telephone – most of us make or receive many telephone calls during the day. Some ideas that may work for you include:

- Try to allocate a specific period during your working day to make all your outgoing calls (although in reality whether you catch everybody that you want to speak to may make this unrealistic).

- Prepare before making any outgoing calls. Have all the details that you may need at your disposal.

- When making an outgoing call, if you cannot get hold of who you want to contact, try and arrange for them to ring back at a specific time so that you can allocate your own time accordingly.

4) Attendance at meetings – the subject area of meetings is covered elsewhere, although in the context of self time management it is definitely worth raising the following points:

- Do you personally need to attend the meetings that you do?

- Do the meetings you attend *add any value* to your day-to-day activities?

- Do you need to have a meeting at all – are there any other alternatives?

- How long do these meetings take – is the time allocated to each of your meetings used effectively? For example, is there a very structured agenda, are all attendees prepared for the meeting beforehand, does the chairman actively and fairly *chair* the meeting, and so on?

- Is it possible that one of your colleagues could go to the meeting on your behalf?

5) Paper management – paper, paper, glorious paper!! The amount of reading and paper that hits our desk on a daily basis is relentless, and if each of us are not careful we can be submerged by the sheer volume. One golden rule which is easier to say sometimes than to achieve is to *HANDLE EACH PIECE OF PAPER ONLY ONCE.*

If you are a *paper generater or shuffler* or like to see your *in-tray* piled as high as a sky scraper, it may well be that serious action is required to help you manage your time more effectively.

There are *four Ds* that we could all aspire to:

- Do it (i.e., *now!*).

- Delegate it.

- Diarize it.

- Dump it (i.e. get rid of it *now!*).

6) In most organizations and business units everybody is busy these days and there is a high emphasis on *getting it right first time*. Nevertheless even with everybody being so busy there is always time to spend time on rectifying errors. It is surely much easier to avoid mistakes in the first place. Paying attention to detail, being clear about what needs to be done and asking for help as necessary may well be a way forward here.

7) Time can also be saved by making sure right at the outset what it is that you are doing. All of us need to be clear about what we are trying to achieve, how we need to achieve it, and when it is to be achieved by. In a favourable environment of open two-way communication, it should be fairly straightforward to regularly discuss and review progress, seek clarity as required, and make sure (and obtain agreement if necessary) that work is proceeding *on track*.

8) Be efficient with your administration – everybody has many issues to think about during the working day. This means that all of us need to be aware of where everything is, whether it is a piece of work we are working on, it is currently in our *in-tray* or even placed out of sight to enable us to focus on the task currently being completed. Enourmous amounts of time can be wasted looking for missing information.

9) During this section we have mentioned more than once that all of us have the potential to work more efficiently. It therefore follows that all of us have the potential to self-develop and this self-development will not take place unless we allocate in a structured way an adequate amount of time to carry out this activity. As has been hinted at earlier, include every activity that you do on a timetable (or even just a *to do list*) and in the context of regularly reviewing your activities, then stick to what you have planned. Self-development is a key activity that should be regularly undertaken.

10) Delegation is a key skill which is discussed in more detail elsewhere. Briefly and in terms of effectively managing your time, it is a critical skill to understand and apply. Each of us should be spending the vast majority of our time on those activities that are key and critical to the achievement of our priority objectives (and probably can be done only by us personally).

If you have colleagues or subordinates to support your activities, then a rigorous review of your ongoing activities can be undertaken to seek agreement on what parts of your day-to-day role can be effectively delegated to your team.

11) Avoid being caught in the *beck and call* activity trap. This means that you are there for everybody, always available, always interruptable, and genuinely seek to please everybody all of the time. The basic premise behind this may be very admirable, although your aim of meeting your own priority objectives to the required standard and on time becomes less likely in reality by adopting this approach.

12) We now come back to where we started and need to reinforce what effectively managing your time means. The natural beginning here needs to be a self-analysis on what you do with your time during a typical day, week and month. Only by doing this will you have a clear and data-based overview of what you do, and therefore what areas you need to focus on to use your time more efficiently.

Making assumptions about how you spend your time is inevitably misleading and inaccurate.

10.2   Assertiveness

Assertiveness is about expressing what you are thinking about and allowing others to do the same. Essentially, being assertive is saying what you think, feel and need. All people have the right to express themselves, and being assertive means that you, or anybody else, has the confidence to present a point of view. Being assertive is also about speaking directly, with honesty and tact. Being assertive, though, does not mean intimidating other people.

Some benefits of being assertive include:

- Learning to speak your mind clearly and effectively.

- Being able to say *no* without feeling awkward or uncomfortable.

- You can feel better by being assertive.

- On occasions being assertive will help you to improve your relationship with others.

- It will enable you to disagree with somebody without appearing to be hostile.

- It will help you to gain more respect from other people.

So already it is clear that being assertive can have its benefits. Assertiveness can sometimes be confused with being aggressive and we need to be very clear about what the differences between aggressiveness and assertiveness can be.

If somebody is being aggressive it usually means:

- That somebody is demanding rather than asking or requesting.

- Verbal or physical abuse is involved.

- Aggressive people quite often feel angry if somebody disagrees with them.

- An aaggressive person may try to manipulate other people through fear or guilt.

- Aggression often implies the need to win at all costs, and anything other than this approach is a compromise or failure.

Aggression can be caused by some of the following factors:

- If aggressive people feel insecure, they may feel that they need to protect themselves and react strongly if they feel threatened.

- There may be examples where aggressive behaviour can actually produce results, although usually only in the short term. This is possibly true in a sales environment. This may then mean that the manager or team leader concerned would be reluctant (or unable) to give up this particular approach. The long-term benefits, however, of being consistently aggressive for the team leader will be that his or her team will only resent and not respect!

- Some people may be aggressive simply through inexperience, because they are still learning how to express their feelings and emotions.

Clearly, then, communication is a key factor here and can be the distinctive factor between being perceived as assertive or aggressive. The features of an assertive conversation often include:

- The need to be specific when in conversation.

- The need to avoid becoming emotional.

- Usually to stay calm and not be threatening.

- Thinking before speaking.

- Being sensitive and if necessary carrying out the conversation in private.

- Picking your time, ensuring that the other person/group of people are not in body and thought elsewhere.

In many ways it is possible for most people to be aware of the need of becoming, and to become, more assertive. Some of these *learnable* skills are as follows:

1) Be confident with the body language you use. You will need to do things like having a relaxed appearance, and maintaining good eye contact. Avoid appearing aggressive by pointing at somebody.

2) In a conversational meeting when you need to be assertive, ensure also that you are proving to be a good listener. Give your undivided attention to the other person when they are speaking, and give clear indications that you are paying attention and understanding an alternative point of view.

3) Have confidence in yourself, and realize that what you personally have to offer is important. Everybody has something to offer and in this sense, all of us need to be assertive at some stage in order to project to others what we have to offer.

4) Similarly, as well as each of us having something to offer so does everybody else. This means that while we personally need to learn to express ourselves to everybody else, everybody else also has the right to express their feelings and opinions to us. These others, and possibly alternative views, need to be respected.

By being assertive there can be particular benefits. Some of these benefits include:

- Having the ability, where appropriate, to say *no*.

- Being assertive can often enable you to settle a disagreement or conflict.

- You will feel able, again when appropriate, to ask for support, assistance or help.

- This behaviour will help you to give and receive direct feedback – either positive or otherwise.

- It is obvious that all of us are made in different ways, and for each of us different behaviours appear and feel more natural. Some of us, therefore, are naturally more assertive than others although as we have indicated above, it is possible to practise being assertive. As with most things, an awareness of a development need, in this case to improve assertiveness skills, is the first step in doing something about it.

10.3   Stress

In reality almost every situation has some aspect of stress – we need to remember stress can be either positive or negative. Most experts agree that some element of stress is a good thing, in the sense that it can encourage you to solve a difficult challenge, or even motivate you to *go that extra mile* to achieve a specific goal, objective or target. Conversely, too much stress is undoubtedly a bad thing, because it cannot be sustained in the longer term. Early symptoms are tiredness, frustration and perhaps depression, and later on this could lead to both emotional and physical illness.

Just about everybody is affected by stress in the workplace and, remembering that how stress affects someone is very much an individual issue, we need to consider some of the following factors:

● Personality
Individuals who are naturally competitive, very ambitious, or lack patience may be vulnerable to the effects of stress.

● The workplace
Research has shown that some types of job and particular work situations can be more stressful than others.

● Changes in personal circumstances
There are several key events in our lives, which are known stresses. These include a death of a close relative, moving house, moving job, having no job, and divorce.

● Other factors
These include your age, general health and well being, your financial situation and how indeed your feel about the way you are, and about life in general.

It is no doubt that stress is becoming a major issue for organizations; as awareness of this area increases, so a greater understanding of what stress is, is achieved over time.

Some of the effects stress can have are:

● Health problems
These include sweating, nausea, headaches and even difficulty sleeping. In more severe cases, stress can lead to heart problems, high blood pressure, ulcers and even death.

● Accidents
Most studies now show that people who are stressed in some way are more likely to have or be involved in an accident that is caused by an error of judgment.

● Loss of productivity
Stress undoubtedly makes you feel tired, lethargic and devoid of normal energy levels. In most cases this means that you are much less effective in the workplace, you may miss work through sickness and ultimately this can be quite a long-term issue.

● Emotional problems
An individual under stress can become very irritable and short-tempered. Some may also become depressed and withdrawn. There is no doubt that these behavioural changes can potentially disturb and upset relationships in the workplace or at home.

What can be done to reduce stress levels

Look after yourself.
- Regular exercise is essential. Medical advice indicates that this means exercising three times a week for a period of around 20 minutes with a view to raising your heart beat to such a level that you can still carry out a normal conversation. The general view is that exercise is a very good way to relieve tension and keep yourself fit. The sensible advice here is that if you are to embark on a regular exercise programme, have a health check with your doctor beforehand.

Watch your diet
- This means ensuring that you are getting a good and balanced supply of vitamins and minerals, which implies eating fresh fruit, vegetables and dairy products. It is believed that eating good balanced meals on a regular basis is also helpful in reducing stress levels.

Sleep
- There are differing views on the amount of sleep an individual needs. There are some, like Margaret Thatcher, for example, who reportedly sleep for around three hours per night. On average, it is believed that eight hours per night is what is required to enable the body to have sufficient rest to face the challenges of the forthcoming day.

Alcohol and drugs
- Clearly, alcohol and caffeine need to be consumed in moderation. Other non-medical drugs that are taken, often disguise the real issue of stress and in the longer term only make matters worse.

Manage your time
- Use a *to do list* – it is very useful if you write down what it is you need to do on a particular day or during a week. Agree what your priorities are (usually after discussion with your line manager) and what needs to be done with most urgency. Agree also which tasks can be left to a little later on.

Recharge the batteries
- During the day it is very sensible to take a break, say at lunch time, where *best practice* would indicate not only eating your lunch but also leaving the workplace for a short period of time, say by taking a brisk walk.

Be realistic
- None of us is a superman or superwoman, so ensure that you are aware of your own limitations; set personal goals that are both challenging and realistic for you personally.

Avoid procrastination

- There are many great thinkers in the world; in the workplace the reality is thoughts need to be turned into action. This means that we need to be very focused in any thinking or preparation that needs to be done, and to move on as quickly as is realistic to complete the task.

Self-awareness

- People now how they feel, and are the first to appreciate if they feel stressed in any way. It therefore becomes an individual thing to take ownership of how you are feeling, and to do something about it. As we have already mentioned, the implications of denial can be very severe.

In the workplace

- Awareness – if an individual is aware of the stresses in the workplace, this is a major step forward. Time is usefully spent if the workplace stresses are written down, together with their primary causes.

Time management

- There are plenty of training courses available and literature which will help an individual in the workplace to use time effectively. With luck this will maximize the chances of an individual achieving his or her own objectives, and will then facilitate an individual building in the necessary breaks during the day.

Lifestyle

- Once aware, share your problems – it is always useful to discuss any individual concerns, particularly about stress, to a partner, family or friend.

Leisure time

- It is essential, if possible on a daily basis but certainly several times a week, to incorporate some leisure activity. Not only will this be a change of mind and leave you feeling refreshed, it will also break up the day and make you feel good.

Enjoy

- When possible, it is important that you try to participate in something that you actually enjoy. This could be a sports event, going to the cinema, or reading a book, for example.

Self-abuse

- Undoubtedly smoking and caffeine have a detrimental affect on an individual's well being. Smoking has been proved to be harmful and caffeine needs to be taken in moderation. If an individual is suffering from stress, inevitably smoking and caffeine merely worsen the situation.

Personal values

- Everyone should take time to reflect and think what is important in life. This may include family, friends, career and education.

Seek help

- Often family and friends are there to support an individual through difficult times. There is only so far that they can go, because they are not professionally qualified. At this point, an individual may need to seek psychological assistance, or counselling, or medical advice.

Take it easy!

- Relaxation should be an integral part of an individual's daily activities. Such examples include:

  - *Breathing* – medical evidence has proved that taking a few deep breaths, probably with your eyes shut, is an excellent way to relax. This is best done in a quiet and comfortable place, and for maximum value an individual should sit or lie down.

  - *Imagine* – a very easy way to *have a change of mind* is to imagine you are somewhere else. It could be walking in a forest, out on a bicycle ride, lying on a beach or whatever makes you feel that you are in a more calm and peaceful environment.

  - *Short and sharp* – in reality very few people have the chance to take as much relaxation in a day as they would like. Often a short break can be very helpful, maybe by doing some light exercises, stretching, or taking in a few deep breaths.

There is no doubt then that stress has become one of the most serious health issues, and in the workplace, with all organizations seeking to become more and more competitive, there is some inevitability that overall stress levels will rise. The working environment is one of rapid and radical change, and employees are being asked to be ever more flexible, make greater contributions, and work knowing there is no longer a *job for life*. We have already looked at some of the individual things that can be undertaken to reduce levels of stress. Across an organization the elements of an ever-competitive and changing environment will not change. Quite the opposite. There are, however, some areas that an organization can influence, as follows:

- Culture.

- Management style.

- Overworking its employees.

- Adverse working environments.

- Lack of training.

- Workplace bullying.

● Workplace harassment.

The legal perspective

In these days of greater self-awareness, an employer must take action to protect its employees from exposure to stress at work and prevent a claim being made. Otherwise, once the claim is proven, the organization may face a claim for compensation, implying negligence towards it employees.

Relevant and recent legislation includes the Health and Safety At Work Act 1974 and the Management of Health and Safety Regulations 1992 – both of these focus on the need for an employer to provide a safe and healthy working environment for its employees.

Regular risk assessments are essential to ensure that employees are not suffering from any increased pressure or too much change, and that their working environment is safe, healthy and enables an employee to carry out his or her duties in a competent manner.

Some implications of stress

● In 1997 it was estimated that the cost of stress in financial terms to British industry is some £7 billion per year.

● Some figures show that over 60% of work absence is caused by stress-related illness (around 14 million working days per year).

● An increasing number of employees admit taking time off work because of work-related stress.

● There is a general trend in insurance claims for compensation resulting from stress-related problems, with this trend showing an increase of over 90% in the early 1990s.

● Where stress is a major issue for employees, a business undoubtedly suffers by lost time, lost output and contracts, remedial costs, possibly higher insurance, and claims for compensation.

11

CUSTOMER SERVICE

11.1 Enhancing the levels of customer service

Customer service – customer care that is, being aware that the customer is an organization's first priority, has become one of the major issues for businesses throughout the world. In whatever industry we consider, the importance of customer service is critical and, indeed, the qualities of a product (whether tangible or intangible) are often judged by the surrounding customer service issues.

In every High Street, shopping mall and Enterprise Park, there will be many retail outlets selling similar products or services, inevitably similarly priced and being offered in well-designed and customer-friendly environments. The prime differentiator is customer service, the offering of excellent customer service each time a customer *touches* an organization. All organizations are striving to achieve a growth in their customer base and ongoing customer loyalty.

The competitive world in which we live means that all customers have choices. Through the various communications media, and very sophisticated marketing techniques, customers are becoming better informed and aware of what choices are available to them – it is far easier for customers to be selective in their choices of products and services, and actually the incentives for customers to move from one service or product provider to another is increasing. The number of examples is endless and clearly include the world of financial services, the gas and electricity industry, the car industry, and even schools and hospitals.

Customer expectations for service excellence are relentlessly increasing – quite rightly so. Some people look back with fondness to previous decades where they perceive customer service being better than today. The reality was that a small part of the population, the privileged class, did enjoy service excellence, provided by a disproportionately large number of employees.

One of the many challenges organizations face today is how to keep their overhead costs to a minimum (for example, staff, premises) and in an environment where customer expectations are so high. We have seen a rapid, and in some cases radical, growth in customer delivery channels, in which face-to-face interaction is only one option. Technology has enabled the telephone to play a crucial role, instant voice recognition is becoming more popular, and computerized operations provide an alternative (*faceless*) alternative for the customer. Indeed, technology has changed the expectations of both customers and staff, irreversibly and radically.

An organization's relationship with a customer is a very complex one. Superficially, this relationship is about those members of staff on the front line and when they meet the customer face to face. Perhaps some employees who do not have direct customer contact are unaware of the responsibility they have in the overall organizational aim of achieving customer service excellence. These people need to be constantly reminded of their responsibility towards customer service and their responsibilities to their internal customers.

Clearly, then, the customer skills of all members of staff need to be maximized. The behavioural skills of all employees who have direct or indirect contact with customers needs to be continually enhanced and reviewed, with the proper training and support being available. Furthermore, these *people skills* need to be recognized, valued and utilized – for those of us that have been to the Disney Theme Parks, think about those members of staff extensively collecting rubbish. In fact, they are often multi-lingual, provide helpful guidance to those many tourists who are looking for particular attractions, restaurants or even advice. Also think about a receptionist or secretary who has interaction with almost every customer who wishes to contact the organization.

Creating the right impression

In many ways, the image, perceived or actual, that a customer has of an organization is one of the most important factors in determining the relationship that customer will have with the organization. Essentially, an organization's image is intangible, but nevertheless extremely powerful. Generally, for example, most of us will have positive images of organizations such as Virgin, Walt Disney, British Airways, and Next. Alternatively, we may have individual opinions about organizations like the various railway companies, and perhaps other examples of public transport.

Organizations in similar sectors compete against each other for a financial customer base, and need some very sophisticated techniques to show that they put their customers first as the priority. There must, of course, be evidence to show that the stated intentions of an organization regarding customer service are the realities in the High Street. Undoubtedly, each time a customer or potential customer contacts an organization, in whatever way, he or she obtains an impression of that organization and how it looks after its customers. Each *customer touch* gives an impression, positive or otherwise, that reflects upon the image of the whole organization.

It is often the first point of contact that creates that initial perception that can be difficult to change – for example, the way in which you are welcomed into a restaurant, the way in which the receptionist greets you when you are arriving at your hotel, the way in which a member of an organization converses with you, the speed with which an order is delivered to your home, and so on. The list is endless.

The way in which employees behave towards and feel about their customers, whether internal or external, is influenced by the culture of that organization. In simple terms, a successful, dynamic, and customer-focused organization leads to their employees feeling highly motivated, and most likely getting the highest levels of job satisfaction possible from their various roles. These employers and therefore their organization are involved in the circle of success. This means their own higher levels of morale and commitment will lead to better business results, which are achieved by providing higher standards of customer service. With this approach being sustained, the reputation of the organization and its employees for providing customer service excellence will spread – either, perhaps, by word of mouth or through the media. Business volumes will continue to increase and further success is perpetuated. In recent years Virgin, Asda and Lloyds TSB are examples of such successful companies.

What a manager must do to enhance the levels of customer service

It is no surprise to conclude that the manager's role is of prime importance. His or her responsibilities include:

- Recognizing the importance of customer service – delivering service excellence must be seen as a priority throughout the organization and within each manager's area of responsibility. Full, comprehensive and ongoing training support must be available to each employee to continue to develop customer service skills.

- Defining these standards of excellence of service delivery to be aspired to – here, the manager must be a role model and lead by example. At every level it must be made very clear what standards of performance are expected each time a customer comes into contact with an organization. Everybody must be aware what the points of contact are between a customer and the organization, because it is at these points of contact or *customer touches* where the organization needs to set, and exceed, exceptional standards of service delivery. Examples of such *customer touches* include:

  - When a customer enters a shop or business premises.

  - How that customer is received and greeted by, say, receptionist, cashier, telephonist, or perhaps the marketing department.

- Regular customer feedback – must be sought to find out exactly what customers think of the service levels provided, and in exactly what areas could further improvement be made. Regular control checks should be in place where service standards are reviewed and assessed against the given standards endorsed by the manager and the organization.

- Constantly reminding – the critical importance of customer service is inevitable, customer expectations are rising and will continue to rise. It is therefore the role of the manager to relentlessly pursue the priority objective of delivering excellent customer service at all times.

- Making sure the whole team contributes to the customer service ethos – there is no doubt that every team member and every single employee has a role to play in contributing towards the delivery of outstanding customer service.

- Defining excellence – the manager must be able to articulate what excellent customer service is, what it looks like, and how it is achieved. This definition must become part of the organization's identity and life blood with the primary aim of all staff feeling a pride in providing excellent customer service. This approach in itself can have an excellent motivational affect for management, staff and customers.

- Recognizing individual performance – members of staff, individually and collectively, need to contribute towards the goal of providing high levels of service. The manager must be aware of what individuals are doing, and make a point of recognizing success. Managers must demonstrate that they care for their staff and are aware of what they are doing. This approach can then be used by the staff themselves, and will be reflected in in the levels of service their customers receive.

Exceeding customer expectation

This can be done in three main ways:

a) Understanding exactly the product or service the customer requires.

b) Understanding exactly what the customer is looking for from that service or product.

c) Being aware of and understanding what the customer needs and expects from each transaction to make them feel valued as a customer.

It is this last point that can be seen as the most complex to achieve, simply because it is the most difficult to understand. Nevertheless there are some positive contributions we can make in this respect:

- By understanding our customer's body language. Various pieces of research confirm time and again that body language plays the main part in any type of communication between two people. It follows, therefore, the more skilful the members of staff are in understanding the body language of customers, the more proficient an organization can become in understanding customer needs. Members of staff need to understand whether a customer is feeling anxious, defensive, requiring to be spoken to as an equal or to be treated as someone very special.

- By listening to customers, we should be able to understand more clearly what our customers are looking for. It is vitally important that you listen to what exactly is being said, how the message is transmitted, and also what non-verbal messages are being sent (for example, by an aggressive or passive tone of voice). It is, in practice, sometimes quite difficult to communicate verbally to get a message across in the way that we intend.

We need to concentrate totally on what a customer is saying, never interrupting and always trying to see things from the customer's perspective. In a two-way customer conversation, quite clearly the customer should be doing most of the talking. Members of staff need to be patient, responsive and show genuine interest in what is being said and at no stage allow individual emotions to prejudice what a customer is in fact saying.

- Questioning technique can be very helpful – particularly if they are questions to facilitate the customer in providing information, opinion or factual evidence.In a selling scenario when a customer is looking to make a purchase, a member of staff must clearly seek to understand exactly what the customer is looking for. This questioning technique is a key factor in enabling someone to do this.

Areas of potential concern

Inevitably, at some stage an organization has to face up to customer complaints. How an organization responds to customer complaints says a significant amount about the way it feels about its customers' opinions. The easy approach is to have an accessible customer relations or complaints department to enable customers to contact the organization to vent their grief. It is what an organization does with the customer complaint that is the most crucial part. In fact, if an organization responds positively to a customer complaint, then the business may not be lost, and in fact the aim has to be to turn a customer complaint into a compliment.

Similarly, the working environment should be such that members of staff should not feel threatened by a customer complaint even if it is about him or her personally. A customer complaint should be seen as a challenge to overcome, the surface issue to be dealt with positively.

So when managing a complaint there are several, simple principles that must be followed:

- Accept and respect the customer's opinion (even if it is not always right!).

- Listen and let a customer have his or her say.

- Sincerely apologize and do not blame somebody else for the error.

- Look for a solution rather than focus on the complaint itself.

- Try to find what would be acceptable as a way forward for the customer and then seek to exceed the customer's expectations.

- Explain to the customer what will happen. The customer should be clear about what will happen next and will not expect to be let down again.

- Ensure that what you have promised to deliver is in fact delivered. Check up to make sure the required progress and commitments have been fulfilled.

- Be sincere when dealing with a customer complaint; treat your customer as you would like to be treated yourself.

- Pre-empt a complaint. If you know that an error has occurred, let your customer know proactively rather than hope it will not be noticed, or wait for the customer to complain.

Quite obviously staff must never show anger at a customer who complains or be rude. Just the opposite. A complaint must be used as a positive opportunity because it may well be that this complaining customer has highlighted an issue that needs to be addressed. A complaint is invaluable feedback about an organization – in fact a complaint may provide an opportunity for an organization to demonstrate to a customer how good it is.

Providing customer service over the telephone

You will be aware that there are many different customer delivery channels, with face-to-face contact being only one. The telephone provides another dimension by which an organization can communicate with its customers and provide excellent customer service, and there are some basic steps to follow as guiding principles when using the telephone:

- Always identify yourself by name. Ensure the customer knows who he or she is talking to.

- Make each telephone call individual and specifically tailored for the customer to whom you are talking.

- If you are proactively contacting a customer, always check that you have picked a suitable time to call. If so, fine. If not, arrange a suitable time to call back, and call back at that time!

- Remember that your customer can feel your verbal contact on the telephone. The customer will know if you are *smiling* down the telephone or if you are eating, smoking or slouching. Sound genuine and sincere.

- If a call is put on *hold* explain to your customer why this is happening. Give customers the chance to be rung back at a suitable time or, if they decide to remain on *hold*, keep assuring customers that they are not forgotten. A few seconds of silence can sound like an awfully long time to a waiting customer. Once the call is continued thank your customer for waiting.

- If a customer has a call transferred, ensure that they are connected to the right person. It is highly undesirable to transfer customers from *pillar to post* several times before they find the right person they are looking to speak to. If possible, tell the customer who they are being transferred to and try to brief your colleague about this particular customer and his or her needs. This avoids your customers having to repeat themselves.

11.2   Providing a quality service

Over recent years interest in service quality has been rapidly increasing. For some time now most of the successful companies have realized that service quality is *the* crucial factor in determining longer-term commercial success. There are well established external and internal pressures which require both public and private sector organizations to become more customer focused and to thereby develop organization-wide, sustainable service quality programmes.

If substandard service quality is provided there can be the following implications for an organization:

a)   There can be cost implications, as a result of waste of resources, the need to rework, duplication of efforts, and the implied need for more robust monitoring and control mechanisms. We can see that most of these costs are avoidable and ultimately unnecessary.

b) If poor service quality is provided, an organization's image will be negatively affected. A poor image can lead to loss of existing customers and a failure to attract new business. Furthermore such organizations may be unable to recruit and later retain the workers that they would wish to employ.

c) Staff morale can be affected, particularly when poor service is provided and customers then take out their anger and frustration on front-line staff.

At the outset, for any organization or team of managers who are seeking to introduce a philosophy of service quality to their organization, the choice with which they are faced must be quite bewildering.

Within the vast array of options available, we shall consider two main approaches.

Customer service

This approach really focuses on front-line service staff and in particular their developmental areas in terms of their interpersonal and communication skills. This approach looks to develop front-line staff through the provision of training and ongoing support. The fundamental assumption here is that as front-line staff become more skilled in handling customers, service quality will improve automatically.

The reality may be somewhat different because the front-line service staff are only part of the whole equation. In other words, rectifying any deficiencies in front-line staff may solve part of the problem, although it may also be quite limited if the rest of the customer service system does not work effectively. In these circumstances, front-line staff who are better trained and interact more effectively with customers do the best that they can against the background of the rest of the organization carrying on as inadequately, in customer service terms, as before. The organization's customers, therefore, continue to see the front-line staff as the organization itself, and therefore see them as accountable for any aspects of poor service. It is far to easy for an organization to say that its front-line staff should not blame system faults, regulations, the customers themselves, or another part of the organization when faced with a dissatisfied customer – in many ways sometimes these front-line staff have no choice and their actions are understandable if they are working in an environment where they can neither change the rest of the service delivery equation, or absolve themselves from the wrath of the dissatisfied customer.

The blueprinting approach

This second area focuses on the systems and operations within an organization – with this approach front-line members of staff are passive (as compared to the first general approach), mainly providing information as required and implementing the approach once it is in place. This second approach has a fundamental assumption that services can be planned and that customers can effectively be *processed* through the organization's operations. Blueprinting prioritizes the need for efficiency and high output, reliability and low levels of inaccuracy. With this emphasis on the system it is the customers who are required to comply with what the organization can provide, rather than the organization amending its approaches to customer service to meet the needs (perceived or actual) of the customer.

With both of the above approaches there are several ongoing issues:

- Clearly, the blueprinting approach and the customer-service approach could work effectively hand-in-hand, although in reality they are usually introduced at different times and implemented in an un-coordinated manner.

- If different parts of the organization have responsibility for implementing different aspects of this drive on total quality, there may be conflicts in aims and priorities.

- With both of these approaches, ownership, and in some ways ultimate responsibility, is placed on the lower levels of the organization. Senior managers do not have (and in some cases possibly do not want) the opportunity to sponsor such an initiative.

- But with both of these types of approach, there is a need for permanent change, combined with a culture of continuous service improvement – far too often these elements are absent.

Some ways in which to succeed in a quality service progamme

- It seems essential that those at the top of an organization should be involved in a quality service initiative from the outset. Senior management must be seen to sponsor and actively participate in the initiative, together with every one of the line managers and team leaders throughout the organization. It may be that they should also become involved in the planning of the quality service programme itself and, for example, have an involvement in any workshops or training events that are scheduled to take place.

- Steps should be taken to avoid any quality service initiative becoming another *one-year wonder* or one which is not sustained or supported from the centre of the organization, or one to which many in the organization will merely respond by saying "we have seen all this before and it didn't work the last time why should it work this time". Therefore, it makes good sense that all (if realistic) members of staff need to be involved in the initiative from the outset – as many as possible need to be involved in the preparation stages, where their views are sought, their input and ideas welcomed and perhaps they actually become involved in the programme design. Then come *live day* all employees need to have involvement in the launch and the subsequent activities of the quality service programme. An organization launching such a programme should realize that it can be successful in the longer term only if it has *the buy in* of its people, and that the programme can continue to grow and develop with the contribution and support of its people, who add their enthusiasm, expertise, knowledge and ideas along the way.

- The whole of the organization needs to be involved in the quality service programme.

We have already seen that such a programme is not just about front-line staff; it is about the whole organization. This means the quality service initiative needs to touch and involve every aspect of the organization, including, for example, all of the service deliverers (for example, front-line staff either face-to-face or through some other direct customer delivery channel) and all support services (for example, finance, management services and training).

- The quality service programme should have a high profile and positive launch. One effective way of doing this is through a series of workshops which are effectively cascaded throughout the organization. One approach is to have workshops for the top management and then to cascade the workshops right down to the lower levels of the organization. Another way, and possibly the better and more integrated approach, is to have workshops where everybody is invited to attend, although attendees at each series of workshops will include people from all the different parts of the organization, and at all different levels of seniority. This latter approach means that, at the launch, most members of the organization are meeting each other, possibly for the first time, sharing ideas, building relationships, understanding each other's roles and networking. In recent years British Airways and Lloyds Bank have run such a series of quality service workshops.

12

THE MANAGERIAL ENVIRONMENT

Introduction

In this section we shall be considering the appraisal process and in particular the appraisal meetings themselves. I am sure that you are aware that performance appraisal can be a very powerful system if used in the right way. It can potentially help:

- To motivate the appraisee.

- To improve the performance of the appraisee.

- To consolidate the relationship between the appraiser and appraisee.

- To identify the development needs of an appraisee.

- The appraisee and appraiser to agree future action plans for the coming year.

- To identify performance goals for the next appraisal year.

It therefore seems realistic if the main dual purposes of an appraisal meeting are seen as being:

- A two-way conversation between appraiser and appraisee aimed at discussing performance over the past year and agreeing on the standards achieved.

- An opportunity to discuss and agree ways in which performance can be improved in the coming year.

12.1 Appraisal systems

Preparation for the appraisal interview

Clearly, it is essential for both the appraiser and the appraisee to prepare thoroughly prior to the formal appraisal interview. Some organizations have these formal reviews quite frequently, often quarterly and in some cases even more often than this.

Both appraiser and appraisee need to consider three broad areas.

1) To collect factual evidence which can be used to assess performance against any agreed accountabilities, objectives, targets.

2) To both consider about the appraisee's ongoing developmental needs (these not need be solely remedial) and future plans (short-term, longer-term, and within and outside of the current business unit).

3) To plan the appraisal meeting itself.

Best practice usually involves appraiser and appraisee meeting a few days prior to the appraisal *interview* itself.

The main benefits of this pre-meeting are for both parties to clarify what their objectives are, and to be clear about what will be covered in the meeting itself, because either party may wish to add other areas for discussion.

Remember that the appraisal meeting itself should be a two-way meeting, with both appraiser and appraisee being fully involved.

Possible areas for discussion inevitably include:

- A review of the appraisee's performance of his or her main tasks and a discussion on how well (or otherwise!) they have been carried out.

- To identify and agree on the tasks that the appraisee has performed well and consider the reasons for this.

- To discuss and agree which tasks could, and should, have been performed better.

- For both appraiser and appraisee to clearly establish the reasons for any areas of under-performance.

- To discuss the appraisee's role itself and to consider any areas for change and how any agreed changes can be managed.

- To discuss the appraisee's ambitions for the coming year and beyond, with the clear priority of managing the appraisee's expectations.

The structure of the appraisal meeting

How an appraisal meeting runs in practice is partly dependent upon your own organization's cultures, systems and expectations. Wherever you work, it is likely that the following areas should be covered:

- At the start of the meeting ensure that the appraisee is as relaxed as possible. Perhaps spend a minute or two observing any social niceties, indulge in some general conversation, ensure that he or she is comfortable and then chat through the agenda for the meeting itself.

- It is critical that the appraisee is clear that the meeting will be a two-way conversation and that as appraiser you create an environment so that the appraisee can contribute fully.

- Early on in the meeting, the main activities, tasks, accountabilities or objectives for the previous year should be reviewed, with any emphasis being given to previously agreed priorities.

- In most cases the appraiser should start the formal part of the meeting on a positive note with a reference to some good work that has been carried out in the previous year. (Throughout the meeting there should be a mixture of praise and constructive criticism with the balance being appropriate to the individual appraisee's performance.)

- The main part of the meeting will probably cover most of the areas we have mentioned in the section above (preparation for the appraisal meeting) and there needs to be a discussion on each of the main areas, with both appraiser and appraisee establishing some common ground about what has or has not been achieved.

- There should be a discussion on the appraisee's developmental needs (this could mean building on strengths, or focusing on any developmental needs) and the appraisee's career aspirations.

- In recent years there has been an increasing trend to discuss in detail the appraisee's own personal development both for the previous year and that planned for the future.

- A mutually agreed action plan must evolve from the meeting, and specific points of action (for both the appraiser and appraisee) should be documented.

- Agree what happens next – for example, a further review meeting.

- Finish the meeting on a positive note.

Critical communication skills of the appraiser
Listening skills

We already realize that the appraisal meeting is a two-way process, which means that the appraiser *must* listen to what the appraisee has to say. Listening is not an easy skill, and some of the main criteria to apply this skill more effectively are given below:

- Do not interrupt the appraisee.

- Remember it is not always appropriate to *break a silence*, it may well be that the appraisee is taking a little time to formulate responses or ideas.

- When appropriate, ask questions to check your understanding.

- Take notes.

- Be fully aware of your own body language. For example, do not cross your arms, look forward, or tap your fingers.

- Do not assume that you know what the appraisee is thinking or is about to say.

- Total concentration is essential.

- Always have good eye contact with the appraisee.

- Be aware of the appraisee's tone of voice and his or her own body language. There may be some contradictions between the words that are being said and the body language.

Questioning techniques

There are many different types of questions that can be used in appraisal interview, and several of these are mentioned below:

- *Open questions* This type of question requires more than a one-word answer from the appraisee, and encourages a two-way discussion to evolve. For example, "what exactly did you do to manage your deputy manager so effectively in the last year?"

- *Closed questions* These are usually answered by the appraisee in a few words. This type of question can be used to clarify information or specific data. For example, "what exactly was your productivity rate for the last month?"

- *Reflective questions* These are used to check your own understanding of what the appraisee has just said. For example, "so from our discussion so far on your sales performance, you feel that a key factor was the lack of support that you received from me?"

- *Hypothetical questions* These can be used by the appraiser to check whether the appraisee understands a particular procedure. For example, "what would you do if we had a situation requiring an emergency evacuation, to ensure the safety of yourself and your team?"

- *Leading questions* These only have one *right answer*, usually being the one that you want to hear! Clearly, this type of question is not appropriate in an appraisal interview. For example, "you have checked the balances on your own accounts, haven't you?"

Questioning

This is giving feedback.

Feedback is any communication, verbal or non-verbal, which offers the appraisee in this case information and guidance about how they behave and the effect that they have on other people.

Feedback can be in the form of praise or constructive criticism.

The guiding principle for feedback is that it should be open, honest and appropriate – it is an opportunity for appraisees to learn more about themselves, what they do, how they do it and the impact their actions have on others. This feedback should help appraisees to improve their overall job performance.

In terms of the appraisal interview, all the feedback from the past year's performance should not be saved up until then! Obviously, feedback should be given on an ongoing basis, and specific feedback given close to the event to which it refers. It may well be that the appraisal interview itself will include a summary of all the ongoing feedback that has been shared with the appraisee during the preceding year.

It therefore follows that when possible the emphasis should be given on positive feedback, which will reassure the appraisee and give encouragement that he or she is performing appropriately and motivate him or her to higher levels of performance. Over time, the appraisee will learn to focus behaviour and job performance around those aspects that have been recognized and praised – this can be particularly important for the more inexperienced members of your team.

Furthermore, if praise and recognition is never given, and the overwhelming emphasis is on criticism, one obvious outcome may be for the appraisee not to risk taking any initiatives and devote energy to learning on what *not* to do. A *play safe* workplace will evolve because the fear of being criticized will exist and the desired culture of continuous improvement will be one that will be very difficult to achieve in this environment.

Some features of positive feedback are as follows:

● When your appraisee has done something well do not forget to say so! Do not assume that the appraisee knows that he or she is doing a good job.

● Always look the appraisee in the eye when you are giving praise to show that you are both being sincere and giving your full attention.

● When giving feedback be specific, and include dates and any evidence that you have.

● Try and place the positive aspects of the appraisee's performance in terms of biggest benefits for the whole team or business unit.

● Pick the right time and place to deliver positive feedback. It may well be that the appraisee would be highly embarrassed to receive such feedback in front of the team.

At the appraisal interview itself, there should really be no surprises for the appraisee because during the previous year the appraiser and appraisee should have dicussed job performance on an ongoing basis. In this context, it makes it even more important that feedback given is always honest – this means that any constructive criticism needs to be delivered to the appraisee as soon as it is realized that performance is falling below the agreed expectations. By addressing any areas of concern immediately, it will enable the appraisee (with the appraiser's support) to take corrective action sooner rather than later.

When an individual is not reaching the required levels of job performance

The ideal situation for any business manager is that all members of his or her team are well motivated, start to make their own contribution towards achieving business objectives and are clear about the purpose of their job.

In reality, there will be times when a member of a team does not perform to the required standards, and it is essential that any instances like this are identified early on and dealt with immediately. The whole team may be looking to the unit manager to act quickly, otherwise the manager's authority will be undermined. If any individual is underperforming, there will be immediate effects on the rest of the team, including increased workloads, possibly a decrease in overall productivity, and inevitably lower levels of morale.

In today's world of headcount constraints, increase in workloads, and more demands being placed upon individual employees as we try to achieve greater levels of performance through a constant environment of change, the expectation is that every employee performs to the required standards. Clearly people should be aware of what is expected from them, and to facilitate this they should be receiving regular appraisals and feedback on their performance. Coaching, training, and guidance from colleagues and management should also be available to facilitate each individual's ongoing development.

It therefore follows that when an individual is underperforming, not only must the issue be dealt with promptly, but also in as fair a way as possible and realistically the individual concerned should be given every opportunity to perform effectively. The manager and the individual colleague should be there to help create an environment where each individual can perform effectively – by implication, therefore, if an individual continues to underperform after all reasonable attempts have been made to provide support and guidance, then formal disciplinary measures may be evoked.

Identifying an individual's performance problems

Performance problems may arise because of an individual's lack of motivation, inappropriate attitude, perhaps being in the wrong job, where an individual needs further training or development or perhaps due to a change in an individual's personal circumstances.

The more obvious indications of such circumstances may be reflected in a decline in an individual's quality of work, a reduction in levels of productivity, a change in attitude, conflict with colleagues, or regular lateness or absenteeism.

The reason for a decline in an individual's performance may not rest with the individual. There may be other issues to consider, for example:

i)   No support being received by the business unit manager.

ii) Stress.

iii) A lack of motivation.

iv) Insufficient training being provided.

v)   An individual not being clear as to what the job entails and what the job priorities and accountabilities are.

The situation in which a manager is placed may not be straightforward, and it could be that one of his team is faced with a complex scenario involving several of the factors mentioned above.

A manager must seek to rectify any decline in performance as soon as possible, and wherever possible before making the disciplinary process inevitable. This means, once the nature of the decline in performance has been specified, a plan to help the individual improve must be set in place. The employee concerned needs to be very clear about what is expected in his or her day-to-day job activities, what the required standards of performance are, and crucially what will happen if the level of performance does not improve and meet the required levels.

Both the manager and employee concerned must be very clear about the issues being addressed, and why an improvement in performance is necessary. Ongoing coaching, counselling, training and guidance, as appropriate, should be made available – regular progress review dates should be agreed, and probably targets or measurable improvements in performance should be agreed. Depending on the nature of the case, the level of improvement in performance required, type of work being undertaken, and the amount of experience the individual has in the role, a realistic timescale should be agreed for the required level of performance improvement to be achieved.

Once the support for an individual is in place, the probable eventual outcomes are as follows:

- The individual's job performance returns to a satisfactory level. Clearly, once the manager concerned is satisfied that this is the case, the individual employee should receive confirmation of this. Any necessary coaching and support should continue to be made available to avoid recurrence.

- It may be agreed between the manager and the employee concerned that the period of *recovery* be extended for a further period. During this further period of time, further training and support should be provided – ideally the length of this extension should be agreed and pinned down to a specific timescale.

- If the individual concerned continues to underperform it will be necessary to begin formal disciplinary proceedings. Before doing so, it should be ensured that all realistic attempts have been made to provide the opportunity for the individual to perform to satisfactory levels and that complete and accurate documentation has been kept throughout.

Employee misconduct

Essentially, misconduct is when any of an organization's rules or accepted standards of behaviour are broken. Examples include non-compliance with legitimate instructions, negligence, offensive behaviour or various types of harassment.

Instances like this are often difficult to manage, primarily because they are usually not specific and clear cut. A manager managing an instance of misconduct must ensure that he or she collates all available evidence, and if possible, considers what has happened in previous similar cases (Personnel may be sought for advice here). Eventually, and clearly as quickly as possible, it must be decided whether an individual's behaviour has actually constituted misconduct and if so how serious it is and whether formal disciplinary action is required.

Quite clearly any form of misconduct must be identified and dealt with immediately. Hopefully this will mean:

- An early resolution to an instance of misconduct before it develops into anything even more serious.

- The effects of misconduct upon the rest of the team are kept to a minimum.

- The individual concerned is not left feeling he or she has *got away with it*.

- The appropriate support, guidance and counselling can be made available to the individual concerned as soon as possible.

- Clarity can be provided to the individual concerned to give every opportunity to return to the required levels of performance and to avoid any repetition of the misconduct.

Key factors for a manager in deciding how to respond to misconduct

a) How serious is the misconduct?

b) What support and guidance have been given to the individual concerned?

c) What penalty/reprimand would be appropriate to ensure that no recurrence occurs?

d) Are there any outside factors that need to be taken into account?

e) What, similar cases have occurred, and how have they been dealt with?

f) The level of awareness the individual has of the misconduct and to what level he or she is able to react positively to any remedial action.

g) The employee's previous track record.

h) The effect the employee's misconduct has had on the rest of the business unit, colleagues in particular.

i) Whatever the details are of a particular case, the primary objective is to ensure that the individual has every opportunity to return to accepted standards of behavior as soon as possible.

12.2   360° feedback

Many organizations are now using the 360° feedback process as a way of developing their employees. This process involves people, usually a manager, being appraised by their colleagues, namely their team, peers and other managers. In addition, the individual concerned usually has the opportunity to fill out a self-assessment and compare his or her own views with those of colleagues. This approach is still relatively new in the United Kingdom, although it has become increasingly popular during the 1990s.

Originally, this approach was intended to be a way of developing an individual and was possibly included as part of a training course or developmental event for a member of the management team. However, this process has now evolved and in many organizations is part of the ongoing appraisal system.

In theory this 360° feedback approach should be offering a more rounded view of an individual's (manager's) contribution to the business, simply because more views are sought. This compares to the traditional appraisal approach in which the manager is topped down, liable to the *halo* or *horn* effects. It is also felt, in these early days of the new approach that 360° appraisal will be a more powerful way of giving feedback and therefore facilitating behavioural change for the appraisee.

Possible concerns with the 360° appraisal include:

- The reliability of the feedback. It may be that some individuals who are giving the feedback, most likely a team member or possibly a peer, may be reluctant to be totally honest either because they are playing some sort of *political game* and feel they ought to say the *right thing* or they do not work in an environment of open and honest two-way feedback.

- Those being appraised may be reluctant to accept the feedback or, alternatively, just prior to the assessment process beginning, managers may well try to influence the process by behaving in a particular way.

- The actual objectivity of this newer appraisal process also needs to be questioned. We already know that more sources of feedback are sought, although it is very likely that each of these sources could be liable to the same possibility of being biased as with the old appraisal system.

- It is possible that the purpose of this 360° process may affect the way in which feedback is given. For example, one of the appraisers, whether a team member, peer, the appraisee's manager, may respond differently if the feedback is to be given for developmental purposes, or as part of the formal appraisal process (and therefore influencing pay awards and possibly future career).

As, and if, this appraisal process becomes more popular there are some areas that will need to be developed over time, as follows:

- If an organization has a formal appraisal process, and 360° appraisal is a part of this, individuals will not have the option to opt out of the appraisal.

- One of the dangers of any appraisal process is the associated bureaucracy and paperwork. Particularly in larger organizations, with a 360° appraisal process, the potential for a bureaucratic *cottage industry* growing alongside it is increased.

- A policy about who actually would, or should, be an appraiser in a 360° appraisal process would need to be established. In some organizations, if this process is for an individual's development, the individual concerned can select his or her own colleagues to give feedback. If the process is part of the formal appraisal system, it is unlikely that this option would be available.

- In traditional appraisal systems, the appraisee's manager together with the appraisee have sat down and discussed what follow-up action is necessary after the appraisal. With 360° appraisal, while it is still more likely that the appraisee's line manager would have the same role, this is not necessarily the case.

The whole evolvement of this 360° system will be a learning process. We have already mentioned that an environment of trust needs to exist in order for honest and realistic feedback to be given and therefore be of benefit to the appraisee. The whole process potentially multiplies the possibilities for an appraisee to be receiving feedback on performance that is biased or being provided by several rather than one appraiser who may be making ill-informed judgments.

So in brief conclusion, while the 360° appraisal process is relatively new, potentially it can be of great benefit to those individuals concerned, and therefore to an organization itself. There are, however, many areas that need to be considered, which are broadly the same as those concerns in the traditional appraisal process, but are multiplied because of the number of appraisers that are now involved in the process.

12.3   Flexibility in the workplace

The working world is becoming ever more complex and competitive. Organizations are therefore competing against each other in their respective marketplaces in order to survive. One of their main priorities is to become more innovative and flexible in meeting the demands of customers and exceeding their expectations. It is widely accepted that the same principles also apply to staff.

More and more organizations are trying to combine meeting the needs of the business and their people by introducing more flexible working patterns that will both attempt to cater for the wide variety of staff needs and continually improve the highest possible standards of work efficiency and customer service.

Increasing flexibility in a workforce, therefore, seems an ideal way to both meet the ever-changing needs and requirements of any customer base, and the variety of circumstances that affect members of staff outside of the workplace. These ongoing changes may well help to improve customer satisfaction, increase business competitiveness and be well received by staff.

Some options include:

Members of staff working reduced hours

This means that salaries, paid leave and staff benefits, where appropriate, are applied on a pro-rata basis, depending upon the actual hours worked. There is much flexibility here, because an individual's working hours can be combined into a few days, spread over a week or combined to give one longer period of work followed by a block of time off (this may be suitable for working parents).

The concept of members of staff working reduced hours will not appeal to everybody, although it is vitally important that organizations make these *part-time* members of staff feel that they make a productive contribution to the business.

Key business benefits of reduced working hours include:

- Giving the manager increased flexibility by allowing some extended hours and/or greater flexibility at the more busy times.

- Members of staff who work in this way often feel that they can contribute in a more focused manner while they are at work.

- Most research shows that among those members of staff who work reduced hours, absentee levels are much lower and punctuality tends to be much better. In addition, these members of staff have a greater opportunity to manage their work and personal responsibilities in a way that is best for them. In time, if it is right for the business and for the individual, it may be possible to evolve a reduced hours role into a full-time position.

- In terms of job design, it may be that some particular functions in a business unit only warrant part-time support. This does not in any way undermine the important of such functions.

- This option also enables those members of staff who wish to pursue, for example, further education, to return to work on a more gradual basis after an extended period away from the workplace, or to work fewer hours prior to retirement, or to feel that they have a critical role to play in the achievement of business objectives.

Issues to consider

One of the main benefits of enabling staff to work on a reduced-hours basis is that an organization can keep skilled staff who might otherwise have left.

Some issues to consider are as follows:

- If a job does change from being a full-time one to a reduced-hours one, perhaps the job can be re-designed with some of the responsibilities being reallocated, out-sourced or even withdrawn (i.e., considered no longer necessary or to add value).

- It may well be that not all jobs are suitable to become undertaken on a reduced-hours basis. Roles that are involved in projects, for example, or those that require minimal supervision would usually be particularly appropriate for reduced hours.

- The impact on others of creating a reduced-hours role must be considered. A manager must reallocate any tasks or responsibilities with care because it could lead to overworked colleagues elsewhere. The whole process must be managed carefully and sensitively.

- The business unit manager and the individual who is commencing a reduced-hours function should jointly discuss and agree an arrangement that meets both the business needs and the personal needs of the member of staff.

- As part of this arrangement, the manager and the individual concerned must both then discuss and agree realistic and specific job responsibilities for the new reduced hours. After this, acceptable workloads must be agreed, as will levels of performance.

- Obviously, reduced-hours staff are not in the business unit all of the time and it needs to be ensured that they are involved fully with the ongoing business unit's activities, and communicated to as effectively as if they were full-time members of the team. If possible and realistic, meetings, for example, should be arranged when reduced-hours members of staff are able to attend.

- Similarly, members of staff working reduced hours must have access to ongoing training and self-development opportunities.

- As part of the dual aims of meeting both business and personal needs as a factor in the reduced-hours arrangements, ultimately the business unit must be able to call on reduced hours members of staff when it needs them most. Ideally, a reduced-hours member of staff should be able to complete those hours when they are needed the most. This may imply some element of negotiation and flexibility and mean that schedules are regularly reviewed and adjusted, if necessary.

Job sharing

This is essentially dividing the responsibilities of a full-time position between two members of staff. This therefore means that the business will get the full-time equivalent for the particular job where this approach is applied, and that two members of staff can benefit from effectively working reduced hours.

The key benefits of job sharing include:

- In the same way as for reduced-hour workers, members of staff who job share are often able to focus on their duties to a greater extent working in this way.

- This approach means that staff can still contribute effectively to what is essentially a full-time job, while working on a reduced-hours basis.

- Again, as with reduced-hours working, punctuality appears to be improved, and absentee levels seem to be lower.

- This option is generally very well received by employees and is seen as a valuable option.

- Some research shows that job sharing may often bring complimentary skills, higher levels of commitment, and staff feel more determined not to let each other down than may otherwise be the case. This *may* give the opportunity for higher quality of work to be achieved in *some* circumstances.

Issues to consider

Ideally, the key factor in a successful job share arrangement is the compatability of the two job sharers in terms of their working styles, skills and probably personalities. This can mean that two members of staff who have worked together previously, or know each other very well, may be the best candidates for this arrangement. Some key considerations when introducing job sharing are:

- Probably not all jobs within a business unit are suitable for job sharing. The manager and the individuals involved need to think about whether a job can be realistically split into two parts. Similarly, what impact would this division have on internal or external customers? Alternatively, does this job sharing possibility give an opportunity to consider a different way of carrying out these various roles of the job and actually enhance the overall job performance?

- It therefore follows that any discussions about a job sharing arrangement must be carefully discussed and communicated between the manager, the individuals concerned, and possibly HR.

- Within any agreed job sharing arrangement, it may be that either of the job sharers may wish to rearrange business and personal commitments in order to attend any critical meetings or arrangements.

- The manager of the business unit needs to be constantly aware of how the job sharing arrangement is working and periodic reviews should be undertaken.

- Job sharers, in a similar way to reduced-hours workers, should not be excluded from any communication issues or from the chance to develop their careers. In reality, both reduced-hours workers and job sharers must be more conscious of the ways in which to raise their profiles when they are at work.

- Clearly, a job sharer's role is dependent on having a successful partnership. Between the two individuals involved, both need to consider what skills that they can contribute, and hopefully the right partner or either of them will have the skills needed to fill any gaps.

- It may be that the working week can be equally split very simply between the two job sharers. This is not always the case, and may mean that both job sharers need to ensure that all the combined responsibilities of the *full-time role* are covered consistently and fairly. Each partner needs to communicate regularly and effectively with the other, and of course keep the other informed of all aspects of job activities. Another option is for each job sharer to be responsible for distinct parts of a role and then between the two job sharers the totality of the *whole job* is covered.

Variable-hours working

Variable-hours working is becoming increasingly important as an option which allows staff to vary the time they start and finish work, while in totality working a standard-length day.

Some options of how to apply this principle of variable hours working include: firstly, an individual selecting and agreeing, with management, one regular start time and finish time and keeping to this (the start and finish times will be different to the *regular hours* of colleagues); secondly, these variable hours could be (and probably should be) regularly reviewed by both management and the individual concerned to meet the changing needs of the business and of their domestic circumstances; some individual's variable hours could be different every day if appropriate to the business needs and the individual's own requirements.

Some probable benefits of variable-hours working include:

- As with reduced-hours workers and job sharers, it seems that variable-hours workers also have fewer periods of absence from the office due to sickness or illness and seem to be more satisfied in what they do.

- By working in the knowledge that they are working hours to fit in more smoothly with their outside commitments, individuals working variable hours can focus more effectively while at work.

- These days technology and global business demands mean that organizations must be open for longer hours every day. Members of staff who are prepared to work variable hours enable the potential for technology, for example, to be utilized for longer periods of time and therefore to begin to become more cost effective.

Issues to consider

These include:

- A manager must try to achieve a balance between satisfying the demands of the staff and the business unit. This means that staff need to be available to cover peak workflows and highest levels of customer demand. It is ideal if any variable-hours schedules can be used to complement these peaks and troughs of workflows and customer demands.

- Not all jobs are suitable to be carried out on a variable-hours basis. Sometimes variable hours may mean staff working without any or with less supervision.

- Ultimately, staff working on a variable-hours basis must realize that business needs come first and that the levels of performance that is expected of them are the same as that of their colleagues who are working traditional hours.

- It may be that the business unit may chose to discuss and agree minimum or core hours when all staff must be present. These core hours must be clearly thought out and fully recognized and accepted by all members of staff as being critical to the success of the business and to the success of any variable-hours policy.

- The type of people who would be good potential variable-hours workers include those who have good time-management skills, are comfortable making decisions and who can work with limited or no supervision. In addition, an ideal variable-hours worker has a high level of self-motivation and is committed to giving his or her best and to contribute effectively towards meeting business goals.

Staff working from different locations

Several possibilities are available here, with members of staff splitting their working hours between the office and working at home or at another location other than the main office/place of work.

The main business benefits are similar to those expressed earlier under the other options available to staff, and additional benefits include:

● It may be that adopting this option means reduced premises costs for a business. Ultimately there may be a need for less office space and lower overheads as a result.

● This arrangement may suit disabled staff, who may be able to work more effectively and with greater comfort from home.

Issues to consider

Again, some of the issues to consider are similar to those considered previously with other flexible working arrangements. Additional areas to remember include:

● If members of staff are working at home, duplicate equipment may be required.

● Any members of staff who are working from home should ensure that they have the capacity to work privately and have the necessary equipment and resources (especially those that are not provided by the business) so that they can be at least as productive as if they were working in the office.

● Staff working under this arrangement may need to be flexible and adjust their schedules if they are required to attend meetings, training or any other activities.

● Clearly, the manager of the business unit needs to ensure that any members of staff working from home are managed as effectively as the on-site staff. They need to be fully involved in any work-related issues in the same way as other members of the team.

● Ideal candidates to work from home are those members of staff who are self-resourcing, who have previously delivered good business results and are self-motivated to achieve results effectively. In addition, these members of staff need to be able to work without close supervision, and to communicate with colleagues mostly over the telephone (although clearly other options will be available in years to come).

When we have looked at these various options, several themes have emerged which will help to make such flexibility in the workplace successful.

Both management and the staff involved should have a focus on achieving business results, and to all be aware of what clear and measurable business objectives need to be achieved. The ways in which management and staff communicate needs to be planned carefully. Shared diaries, e-mail, voice mail and written communications all play a crucial role. Whenever flexible working options are introduced, the impact of such arrangements needs to be carefully thought through, particularly with regard to external and internal customers. Such proposals are still relatively new to organizations, and in this respect they need to be regularly reviewed and possibly amended over time to ensure that the maximum benefit is achieved for both the business and the members of staff.

12.4   Health and safety

All aspects of health and safety are related to the protection of employees and for any other individuals who are affected by what the organization does. The health and safety programmes or policies also apply to people or individuals who may be visiting the organization, for whatever reason.

Safety programmes are primarily focused on preventing accidents, with the clear aim of minimizing any resulting loss or damage to individuals and premises. The programmes inevitably relate more to systems and procedural aspects of work than to the working environment itself – as with health programmes, safety programmes are primarily concerned with protection against hazards of all types.

Health programmes concentrate upon the reaction of employees to their working environment.

The guiding principles of health and safety

1) In most cases, there is some inevitability that any accidents or industrial issues will be complex in themselves but ultimate arise from some aspect of faulty management or leadership. In practical terms this may mean having ineffective health and safety policies, or inadequate health and safety training.

2) In any health and safety programme it is vitally important that any potential hazards are identified, and that any necessary safety and protective equipment and measures are available and maintained. Furthermore, it must be the case that prompt and effective remedial action is taken should any health and safety issue arise. This usually means that there needs to be a system for reporting accidents, the provision to have regular safety checks and possibly regular inspections, that all safety equipment is regularly, rigourously and effectively maintained and that aspects of health and safety are given a real priority by managers and team leaders.

3) Senior executives and top management should be seen to take an active interest and involvement in aspects of health and safety. They should take an ongoing and personal interest in ensuring that various policies and practices are effectively carried out.

4) Following on from 3) above, senior managers, and all levels of managers and supervisors in the hierarchy, must have and retain full accountability for implementing, endorsing and applying all aspects of health and safety within their areas of responsibility.

5) A thorough and ongoing programme of training and education should be available for all employees on all aspects of health and safety.

The Health and Safety at Work Act 1974

This was the most recent legislation on health and safety and has been followed by further related acts in the 1980s. This act required that all organizations have a written statement of their health and safety policy and must make sure that all employees are aware of this policy.

These health and safety policies should be visible to all employees, by being placed on notice boards, or by being available, say, in booklets or brochures for all employees.

These health and safety policy statements consist of three main parts:

- The general policy statement.

- How the health and safety policy will be organized.

- How the policy itself will be actually implemented.

Within this policy statement it will be clearly stated that the safety of all employees and any members of the public associated with the organization, directly or indirectly, is of absolute importance. Furthermore this policy statement will confirm that the requirements of the act will be implemented in practice as well as in principle. This policy statement will also confirm that senior management will be ultimately responsible for every aspect of health and safety within the organization itself. The various levels of management throughout the organization will have their own areas of accountability for health and safety within their own spans of control.

The roles of managers and team leaders in health and safety

The main aspects to be considered here for managers and team leaders are as follows:

- To develop health and safety policies and procedures.

- To then ensure that these health and safety procedures are carried out across their areas of responsibility.

- Managers and team leaders must provide colleagues, as appropriate, with the necessary assistance, training and guidance that they need in order to ensure that these policies are carried out effectively.

- Information and control systems must be set up so that health and safety activity can be rigourously monitored and performance based on fact rather than perception. Clearly, any deviation from the policy requirements must be quickly identified and rectified.

- Those managers and team leaders who have direct responsibility for team members must constantly observe to ensure that the policies are being carried out.

- Managers and team leaders at all levels should be supporting each other to ensure that they are helping each other to fulfill their own requirements, at different levels, in implementing the health and safety policies.

12.5   Managing absence

In every organization there are times when an individual is unable to attend work. In the vast majority of cases, members of a team are absent only when necessary. As with everything there are exceptions, when the frequency of an individual's absence from the workplace will cause concern to the team leader or manager about either the conduct or the ability of the individual to satisfactorily carry out his or her role and responsibilities.

Absence from the office may be due to a number of reasons – some examples include sickness, family problems, work-related reasons. As a manager or team leader, we are aware that anybody's persistent absence from work, however genuine, does inevitably disrupt the day-to-day activities of the business unit. Inevitably, if somebody is absent from the workplace the pressure is placed upon other members of the team and implies additional costs. Absence from the workplace is therefore something that must be proactively managed.

If nobody at managerial or team leader level is aware of who is absent from the office, and the whole issue is poorly handled or even worse ignored, over time feelings of resentment, demotivation and discontent may well start to emanate not only from those who regularly attend the workplace but also from those who have been absent.

Guiding principles

As a manager or team leader, it is very important that you ensure that team members are aware of their responsibilities when they are not able to go into work.

- You should try to reach the situation that when any of your team is unable to attend work, he or she should be contacting you as soon as possible on the first morning of absence from the workplace. When possible you should try and take the call personally or nominate someone to take these type of calls on your behalf. Clearly, it may not be possible for the individual to make contact with you directly due to a particular type of illness. It may then be that somebody will ring on their behalf to let you know what is happening.

- If possible, and if known at the time of the contact with you, employees should be able to inform you what the problem is. If known (if they have received confirmation from a doctor, for example) they should let you know why they are away from work and ideally how long they expect to be away from the workplace.

- It is usually standard practice that if an individual is going to be away ill for more than seven calendar days (including weekends), a doctor's certificate is required as confirmation. Prior to this seven-day period, an individual member of your team is able to self-certify his or her absence. If the period of absence away from the office extends beyond the seventh calendar day, a further doctor's certificate is required.

- As a manager or team leader you should proactively be keeping in contact with any member of your team who is absent from the office unwell. This contact may be by regular courtesy telephone calls or perhaps a visit to his or her home. Clearly, the situation needs to be considered as an individual case.

When a member of your team returns to work after a period of illness

Best practice indicates that when a member of your team returns to work you sit down with him or her on that day. The primary purpose of this meeting is to show your genuine concern for the individual and give reassurance to those who have been away, genuinely ill. It also gives you the opportunity to let people know that not only are you very concerned that they are well enough to return to the workplace, but also that they have been missed.

In terms of parity, and consistency, it is very important that you as manager adopt this practice for all of your team members.

In the context of this meeting, it is always important that you do welcome your colleague back to work. The opportunity should also be taken to confirm the reasons why, using discretion and sensitivity as appropriate, your team member was away – remember, of course, there will be times when an individual will not want to discuss the particular details of an illness with you. If this should be the case, then your Personnel colleagues may need to become involved.

As a manager, you must also be ensuring that the individual is well enough to go back to work. The situation in which returning employees put themselves or their team members at risk could become a very serious scenario. Similarly, it may be that you make a managerial judgement to put your colleague in a very slightly different role in their early days returning back to work, to ease him or her back in to a full day's activity.

Quite obviously, this meeting should not be seen by the individual, or perceived as such by everybody else, as an interrogation. The idea is to show your concern for your team members, not to introduce the culture of a *police state* of suspicion and lack of trust. It is quite often the case these days that business units keep regular and accurate records of sickness and illness because then they are able to quantify the affect and cost of absence to the business . This approach also, if required, gives you the opportunity to observe trends on particular members of your team who *may* be abusing the system.

Managing the impact on the business unit of absence/sickness

In the vast majority of cases, individuals miss work when they are either on holiday or genuinely unwell. There may, however, be situations where this is not the case.

In all cases of sickness or illness, genuine or otherwise, an individual who is away for this reason has an impact on the business unit. Ultimately the day's or week's activities need to be carried out and completed with the reduced resource. Again, treating each particular case individually, people must be made aware of how their absence has affected their colleagues.

When a situation arises where a manager feels an individual is *playing the system*, it is essential to be firm, sensitive and consistent.

In cases where an individual has been ill for a long period of time, it is usually expected for that individual to continue to supply the appropriate documentation to confirm how long they are likely to be away.

In other cases it may be that there is no confirmation of any particular illness where an individual takes regular periods of time off *ill*, and possibly he or she may even be one of your poorer performers. It is in these, hopefully infrequent, sets of circumstances that a specific course of action may need to be taken.

If, as manager, you have these suspicions, then at the first opportunity the reasons for the individual's period of absence need to be clarified. Clearly, every care needs to be taken that any conclusions drawn are based on factual evidence and not rumour, a colleague's opinion or a hunch.

It may be that some type of counselling will be required, possibly from yourself, from Personnel or even from a qualified counsellor.

If it is the case that this level of *non-genuine absence* continues for a particular individual, it is an issue that needs to be managed.

On an ongoing basis you need to continue and try to explore why an individual is away from the office, and try to give what support you can to help this individual improve his or her attendance record. It is often the case that Personnel should become involved now, as the situation may soon be approaching that if an individual is unable to give some clarification to explain the absence, a disciplinary approach may need to be considered.

This level of discipline could either consist of an informal warning, or eventually a more formal approach. Most organizations give an individual the opportunity to improve an attendance record, over a realistic period of time, often up to three months or so. In some extreme cases it may be that the individual concerned will exit the organization.

Treating each period of absence as an individual case

As we have indicated throughout this section, when any individual is away from the office ill, on all occasions this must be treated sensitively and genuinely.

There may also be times when a member of your team is unable to attend work due to other family problems: if one of their children is ill, or if they need to attend a doctor's or dentist's appointment, or need to be away from the office for another reason. As a manager, we all wish to support our team whenever possible, and in the case of family illness, compassionate leave may well be appropriate, as it may be if a member of your team's child is poorly. In the case of doctor's or dentist's appointments, clearly, each individual member of your team has the right to attend. It is always helpful if your team members are encouraged to attend such appointments either at the beginning or the end of a working day if they cannot be arranged outside normal working hours.

Whatever approach a manager takes when managing sickness or absence from the workplace, it must be an approach that is clear and visible to everybody, above all seen to be consistent, fair, and based on actual evidence in all cases.

12.6   Equal opportunity

Background

Equal opportunity has become a key feature in the way in which an organization manages its business and is not only driven by recent legislation. It is possible that an organization will belongs to the following campaigns or working parties:

- *Employers Forum on Disability* – this focuses on work for people with disabilities, currently involving more than 200 companies.

- *Employers for Child Care* – main objective to facilitate organizations' implementing child care policies.

- *Race for Opportunity* – which aims to increase the number of ethnic minorities in a workforce.

- *Opportunity 2000* – whose main aim is to improve the position of women in the workforce.

- *Agenda for Disabled Customers* – which aims to provide the best possible service for the disabled.

Some facts and figures

- With current trends, the number of women are out-numbering the number of men in the workforce.

- Only 4% of company directors are women, with only 2% being executive directors.

- Approximately 6% of the workforce are from ethnic minority groups.

- 6% of the workforce have some kind of disability.

Aspects of equal opportunity for a member of staff
Parental leave

This entitles either parent a minimum amount of leave for the birth or adoption of a child. At the end of this period of time a member of staff has the right to return to the *old job*.

Paternity leave

This enables the male members of staff to take a shorter period of time off from work for the birth or adoption of a child.

Flexible working

This has attained a much increased profile in recent years, and is aimed to help a workforce and individual members within it to achieve a realistic balance between their work and home commitments. Options here include reduced-hours working, job sharing, flexi-time, and homeworking.

Compassionate leave

This option is available to cover unplanned events in which a member of staff, either male or female, needs the support of the business immediately.

Career break

This facility is available to members of staff who wish to take a period of absence away from work, possibly up to 5 years, to look after children up to school age.

Disability

The main provisions here are covered by the Disability Discrimination Act 1996, which made it unlawful to discriminate on the grounds of disability in all areas of employment.

Harassment

Not only includes sexual harassment but also bullying or victimization, with an individual's race, sex, religion, disability or any other reason being the catalyst.

12.7   Part-time staff

Over the past decade the number of part-time staff in employment, or key-timers as they are now sometimes known, has multiplied. A number of staff working on a part-time basis is defined as one who is working less than 35 hours per week. Now approximately 1:5 of the workforce is employed on a part-time basis although the proportion of each organization can vary significantly. Also, the vast majority of part-time workers are women.

Some of the factors that have increased the demand for more part-time or key-time workers includes:

● Legislation.

● The availability of technology which has enabled organizations to reduce costs.

● Customer demand for an organization to be open longer.

Part-time workers enable an organization to have a pool of employees who can be utilized when they are needed. This may mean part-timers working at the busiest times of the week, although most organizations seek to maximize, when possible, the needs and requirements of their part-time workers and also the needs of the business.

Some organizations could not meet their increasing customer demands without the support of part-time workers. For example, in banking, customers are now expecting that newer delivery channels are available all day and every day. This is particularly true in telephone banking and is increasingly so in the branch network.

Also, with the ever-changing and evolving role of families, and parents within them, there has been an increased demand for part-time work. For example, part-time work can suit women with children or working evening shifts can suit mothers whose husbands work during the day.

There are some areas for management to consider when working with their part-time team members. Workflows can be more difficult to coordinate, and it is essential that the part-time team members are also fully involved in any communication processes. It is also very important that all part-timers feel fully included in the wider team activities, and have the same opportunity to feel part of an organization as everybody else. With the increasing numbers of part-timers in many organizations, it is important that these issues are dealt with effectively. Some companies ensure that their part-timers are involved in any major activities, for example, project work or any team events. It seems likely and probably quite obvious that part-timers who are participating in important issues in the workplace generally have a greater sense of belonging and commitment to the organization itself.

Other areas of potential concern include:

- Staff turnover for part-time workers. Although all levels of employee turnover need to be closely monitored, in some areas, for example, central London, it appears that turnover for part-timers is much higher, presumably because there are many more alternative job opportunities elsewhere.

- In the area of incentivization, organizations usually include their part-timers on a pro-rata basis. If the incentives are financial, other than administrative issues, this should present no problems. Issues can arise, if for example you are trying to pro-rata incentives such as company cars or healthcare.

- Legislation has also increased the protection available to part-time workers, for example, the European Union Law Article 119 of the Treaty of Rome. This article makes it illegal for an organization to discriminate against an individual on the grounds of sex either directly or indirectly. As a result, many recent decisions made by the European Court of Justice have found that organizations are indirectly discriminating against part-time workers (as the majority of part-time workers are women). Furthermore, the European Court has also held that part-time workers should be included in sick pay schemes, company pension schemes and that part-time workers who are employed for fewer than 16 hours a week should share the same rights as full-time workers. Now, legislation has been introduced which means that the requirement for an individual to work more than 16 hours a week to establish *continuity of service* has been removed. This means that all employees, including *all* part-time employees, have the same rights in terms of unfair dismissal, redundancy pay, maternity leave, health and safety, and every other aspect.

- In terms of maternity, part-timers who have two years service can return to work after 40 weeks maternity leave. All women in employment, whether full-time or part-time and irrespective of how long they have been in work, have a right to 14 weeks maternity leave. In such circumstances, an employee can return to work after the 14-week period and must be allowed to return to the *old job*. This area is clearly a sensitive one, and is often not straightforward. For example, after maternity leave, a woman may well want to return to work on a part-time basis rather than the original full-time basis. In this event, an organization may well say then that she cannot do this because the job that was left was full-time. Although some organizations are flexible enough to accommodate these changes, the critical issue is whether the employee can justify whether the job that was left still needs to be done on a full-time basis.

● Again as a result of European Union directives, all employees have the right to four weeks annual paid holiday, which is paid pro-rata for part-timers. This piece of legislation also specifies that there should be a minimum rest break when the working day is longer than 6 hours.

The trend for part-time working is undoubtedly increasing, and the continuing onset of computerization of operations, centralization of activities and the constant need to drive down costs, combined with increased customer demand for 24-hour-per-day service, means that the demand for part-time workers will continue to increase significantly.

12.8   Managing disability

Since 1995 the Disability Discrimination Act has made it illegal for an organization to discriminate against disabled people in the context of their rights to access of goods and services. Essentially, disabled people are legally protected from being discriminated against.

There are three main dimensions of this act:

● For employers
The 1995 Act makes it illegal for an organization to discriminate against actual disabled employees or potential disabled employees. There would be an obvious effect on recruitment and selection policies, and ongoing employment policies.

● For service providers
This means that any disabled customer should be able to expect the same level of service as everybody else.

● For premises
Organizations are expected to modify their premises, where appropriate, so that any disabled customer and/or employee has exactly the same ease of access as everybody else.

As with any relatively new act, the wording is crucial. In reality, what the wording of the act means in practice will only be validated by the courts when various *test cases* are brought (probably through an industrial tribunal beforehand).

This Act relates to employees or customers who are disabled. This protection provided by the 1995 Act applies only to those individuals who fall within the definition provided within the Act's words. The criteria include:

● An individual having a physical or mental impairment.

- This disability means that the individual is unable to carry out normal regular day-to-day activities.

- The disability must be long term.

- Examples of factors affecting an individual's ability to carry out regular day-to-day activities include:

  - Mobility.

  - Speech, hearing or sight.

  - Physical coordination.

  - Manual dexterity.

In terms of an organization's recruitment process, since 1995 it is illegal for discrimination to occur in the selection process when advertising the vacancy itself and then in the following recruitment and selection process. The organization also has to consider how it will accommodate its disabled employees on the induction programmes in the promotion and job transfer process, in the provision of ongoing training, and in terms of employee retention and the avoidance of harassment.

According to the 1995 Act, discrimination probably occurs in two main ways:

a) A disabled person receiving less favourable treatment. Essentially this means an organization would treat an employee who is disabled in a less favourable manner than their colleagues who are not disabled. If an organization, in a court of law, is unable to justify this treatment, it would be deemed to have acted unlawfully.

b) Where an organization fails to accommodate an employee with a disability by not making the necessary adjustments to the workplace. Examples of potential adjustments to the workplace include:

  - Making adjustments to the premises.

  - Making arrangements for any specialist training required.

  - Allowing the disabled person time off for any medical treatment or rehabilitation that may be required.

An example of the first instance given above would be if any recruitment process a disabled person who used a wheelchair applied in competition with an able-bodied person. If ultimately and for no valid reason, other than the disabled person using a wheelchair would *get in the way*, and was not selected although in every other way was suitable for the job advertised, it may well be that discrimination has taken place.

In the second instance, if a disabled person does take an organization to court, the court itself will consider how practical it was for the organization to take the necessary measures; the financial implications for the organization to take these necessary measures; what *disruption* may be implied as a result; what, if any, financial or other support would have been or could be made available for the organization to make these adjustments.

12.9 The role of the trade union

There are four main ways that we can consider *union power*:

- *The union's profile* – this is where it is argued that unions operate in an unsympathetic environment, which is usually reinforced by the media, and that therefore the visibility of the activities of the unions is no guide to their power.

- *Industrial power* – one of the main activities of a union is to address (or redress) the balance between workers and employers. It would therefore appear that without union *power*, the balance of industrial relations is stacked heavily in favour of the employer. What this has meant in reality is union activity being evident and visible in certain specific areas: wage negotiations, working conditions and manning levels. There has been no significant role for unions in the location of factories, sales policies and product design, for example.

- *Militancy* – key criteria here are the size, bargaining strengths and industrial militancy of a particular union. Currently, if we were to measure the level of militancy by strike statistics, the United Kingdom is now low when compared to other major industrialized countries.

- *Degree of (perceived) influence on government* – traditionally, the unions have enjoyed a key influence in the decision-making policy of the Labour Party, although in the last year or so this influence appears to be being reduced. More often than not, unions tend to be under pressure from the politicians, civil servants and the media to restrict their demands and avoid a confrontation with government.

We can also evaluate the activities of unions from the political, economic and social perspectives, and we shall now do so looking at each area in turn, accepting fully that each area cannot operate in isolation from the others.

Political

In the United Kingdom in the late 1970s and 1980s, the then Conservative government took the view that the unions with their monopoly power had far to much influence over the free-market mechanism. At that time some saw the unions as being responsible for creating inflation and limiting productivity. During the 1980s many important acts were passed including: Employment Act 1980; Employment Act 1982; Trade Union Act 1984; Employment Act 1988. These acts covered a wide range of matters, which endorsed the government's industrial relations philosophies which included: trade union recognition; union membership and non-membership; unfair dismissal; liability for organizing industrial action, and methods for electing union leaders.

Since, in the UK, a Labour government has recently been elected, it will interesting to see how the government's relations with the unions evolve. As mentioned earlier, it would seem that the once harmonious, cooperative, and interdependent relationship between the Labour government and the unions is changing. Furthermore, there has been a considerable decline in union membership over recent years and a further erosion of the influence of collective bargaining by the significant growth of non-unionized organizations in the newer sectors of the economy (for example, the distribution sector and the miscellaneous services sector).

Economic

In two recent decades, we have seen the 1980s starting off with a severe recession, followed by a period of continuous growth until the late 1980s followed by another downturn in the early 1990s. The recessionary periods saw the ongoing debate between employers, employees and unions over cost, prices and product quality. During these years the concept of *new realism* emerged, which saw the unions' approach evolve which linked costs and profits to job security. In fact, during these years, the fear of unemployment clearly affected and undermined trade union power – generally, members were not prepared to risk their jobs by striking for increased pay.

During these two decades in particular, we saw a radical realignment of the employment structures. There has been a significant decline in the number of manufacturing jobs, and an equally rapid increase in the trend towards the service industry (for example, finance, hotels and catering). There was a concurrent decline in nationalized industries which was driven by the Conservative government and is likely to be further endorsed by the present Labour government. The latest trends in employment show further moves towards self-employment, women workers and part-time workers. The traditional areas of union strength, notably mining, engineering, transport, steel and ship building, continue to decline.

Social

Traditionally, the argument has been that the bigger a business unit, the greater are possibilities for trade union activities being facilitated by a large number of employees, ease of communication, and ease of recruitment and solidarity. Since the 1980s there has been a clear move towards a smaller size of business enterprise, and there has been a concurrent alteration in employee attitudes from collective to individual values. The clear implication has been a reduced commitment to union membership, and therefore a lower propensity to unionize.

Pay was traditionally one of the main areas where unions had a key role to play. Since the 1980s many employers are shifting to a policy of pay determination by de-centralization. Essentially, pay deals are agreed by excluding collective bargaining, and the resultant pay agreements are applied generally to the non-unionized workforce. There was some inevitability in this which was to necessitate the role of the unions changing, and some of the major trends have been as follows:

- A tendency for the unions to approach management to gain a presence in the new work-related environment.

- As a result, usually because of *no strike* agreements, conflict between management and unions was minimized.

- The unions were prepared to play a supporting role for the new forms of work involvement at company level – for example, the introduction of advisory and company counsels.

During this time, the fundamental roles of the unions across both the private and public sectors were changing – their new philosophy became known as *market unionism*.

Other major factors that have influenced the changing roles of the unions in recent years include:

a) The widespread introduction of pay arrangements based upon individual merit or performance (usually known as performance-related pay). The union saw this trend as further undermining the collective payment systems negotiated at national level. Evidently, most unions are now having to accept the existence of PRP, as similar policies have been adopted in the areas of food, retail, textiles, and airports, for example.

b) Some argue that the unions, as an organization themselves, can provide a basis or cooperation in a time of persistent change (possibly revolving around increased competition and flexibility of working practices).

c) Some still hold the view that there will always be a need for a *union voice*, whereby a strong union voice can present and represent views of employees.

d) There has been a relentless focus on labour costs as a percentage of total costs. Automated processes and computerized systems have drastically reduced the numbers employed and radically changed the cost structures in those organizations affected. In all organizations there is an obvious and fierce competition to improve the added value of labour.

    Throughout the TUC, for example, believed that technological change would benefit all parties if unions, management and government planned its implementation in partnership. The reality has been that union activity saw some success in avoiding large-scale redundancies, with most job losses being achieved by natural wastage. The union involvement has been limited overall, and unions have been having ever less involvement in key organizational decisions.

e) Over the past two decades, there have been significant changes in social values, demographic changes, lifestyles and attitudes to work. The main features of these changes have been the continuing fall in the number of young people who are available to the labour market, the increased role of women in the labour market, and the expansion of part-time working.

In conclusion we have seen that there has been a decline over recent years in union activity. The challenges facing the unions have included:

- Ongoing job losses.

- The smaller average size of firm in the UK economy and elsewhere.

- New terms and conditions of employment.

- Workers' fear of redundancy.

- Job security.

- Greater work measurement.

- Changes in working conditions.

Looking ahead, the unions would still hope that the relatively recently elected Labour government would provide a more supportive approach and possibly more supportive legislation. In addition the following factors are also relevant as we look forward:

- Unions may merge with each other to consolidate their power basis.

- Unions will have the opportunity to recruit in the fastest growing sectors of industry, which historically have been neglected by the unions. The realities of achieving this goal may prove somewhat difficult.

- The unions could look to improve the services provided to members, especially by providing financial, welfare and legal support.

- Above all, the unions must look to work in harmony with the employer as their view evolves to be that of the welfare of their members is dependent upon the success of the employer, and that in today's economy the employees' wages and conditions have to be related to the profitability (i.e., ability to pay/afford) of the employer.

12.10 Grievance and discipline

Background

Most organizations these days have a disciplinary and grievance policy which applies to all members of staff. These policies are then supported by guidelines and procedures which enable the policies to be put into place when required.

Best practice in a case of need for any disciplinary procedure to be seen as consistent and fair while being supported by the clear rules which outline these standards of conduct at work, thus making it extremely clear to all employees the parameters within which they are expected to carry out their duties.

Inevitably, the application of any disciplinary procedure carries the threat of *punishment* with it. Ideally, although perhaps naively, this should not be the case – the primary purpose of any disciplinary procedure is remedial and corrective. When any disciplinary procedure is evoked, it is essential that all employees are treated in a consistent and fair way. Local management is responsible for this, and it will normally be the case that Personnel are involved at the outset.

Any disciplinary procedure consists of the following stages, which we shall discuss in greater detail later on in this section:

- Informal warning

- Oral warning.

- First written warning.

- Second and final written warning.

- Gross misconduct leading to exit from the organization.

As mentioned above, Personnel will work very closely with local management in implementingdisciplinary policies, and any action taken in this respect should be accurately documented, whetherthe actions are formal or informal. In addition, on each occasion, instances should be handled as promptly as possible, a full and fair investigation should be carried out to establish the facts and this will enable a consistent approach to be taken.

The informal disciplinary process

This approach should be the starting point for the majority of disciplinary instances. This is because on most occasions, local management should aim to provide coaching and guidance to enable performance improvement from the individual concerned – this will avoid the need for any formal process to be invoked.

Nevertheless, even at an informal level it is critical that employees are made fully aware of what has happened, and that they are given a full opportunity to defend themselves. In any case, before approaching an employee any instance regarding discipline should not be treated in isolation. It must be clearly established what rule or regulation has been broken, how frequently this has happened, and what are the implications/effects on other members of the team or anyone else (for example, customers).

Any informal disciplinary discussion between management and a member of staff *must* be documented, and details kept must include why the meeting was held in the first place, and what remedial action was agreed upon to avoid recurrence. The whole disciplinary process should be clear and visible, and therefore any written record of each event that is being kept by the organization should also be given to the employee.

For the informal disciplinary meeting, examples of employers misdemeanors could include poor timekeeping, unauthorized absences from the business unit, possibly attitudinal problems.

After any informal meeting, a way forward must be agreed upon. It is the responsibility of both local management and the employee concerned to review progress, typically over the following three-month period. Clearly the aim is to avoid any repetition of the misconduct – non-recurrence will often lead to the employee's *slate being wiped clean*, but a recurrence will inevitably lead to the formal disciplinary procedure being put in place.

The formal disciplinary process

From what has been said so far, it is clear that local management must carry out a full and thorough investigation prior to implementing a formal disciplinary proceeding.

Immediately after any full investigation has been undertaken, the employee concerned must be made aware of what is happening. Then at each point of contact regarding this procedure between the employee and local management (and possibly Personnel) the employee has the opportunity to be accompanied either by a work colleague or a representative of a trade union.

Broadly, there are two main types of behaviour requiring formal disciplinary procedure. Firstly, misconduct, for example, poor work attendance or breaching of specific rules and regulations. Secondly, gross misconduct which is an instance so serious that it could lead to instant dismissal for the employee concerned. Examples include dishonesty or violent behaviour.

The four stages of the formal disciplinary process

The oral warning stage

At this first stage, again a full investigation of what exactly has happened must be undertaken. Personnel must also be involved and be kept fully informed of what is happening.

Once it is established that an oral warning is appropriate, the employee concerned must be advised why this is the case together with total clarity about what needs to happen to achieve any remedial action. At this stage, the employee concerned also has the full right of appeal.

At this oral warning stage, a written record must still be kept of the meeting between local management and the employee – this written note will detail why the oral warning stage was invoked, together with exactly what level of improvement is required, in terms of behaviour and what actions by the employee to reach the required standards of behaviour. After an agreed period of time, should the employee's standard of behaviour be satisfactory, then the original note is disregarded. (Typically this period of time would be six months, and if this is the case, local management should confirm this to the employee).

It is also crucial that while the objective of this oral warning stage is to enable remedial action to achieve the improvement in employer behaviour required, if this does not happen then the employee must be aware that the next stage of the disciplinary procedure may well be invoked.

The first written warning

This stage of the disciplinary procedure applies when either the oral warning stage discussed above has not been effective, or if local management (together with personnel) agree that the disciplinary procedure should begin at this stage.

Again, the employee concerned should be kept fully informed of why this stage in the disciplinary process is being applied, the specific nature of the alleged offence and what level of remedial action is now required. As with the oral warning stage, the employee has the full right of appeal.

As at each stage of the disciplinary process a full written record should be kept and, at this first written warning stage, the organization may be looking for a sustained period of improvement from the employee of up to 12 months before satisfactory conduct can be confirmed. The employee must be made fully aware that, if appropriate, the next stage of the disciplinary process will be applied.

The final written warning

This stage of the disciplinary process applies when either the first written warning stage has proved ineffective, or that the nature of the *alleged offence* is so serious that it is appropriate that this stage applies immediately.

The role of local management is similar to that at the first written warning stage – full documentation should be kept and the employee must be made fully aware of the specific allegations, and what needs to be done to achieve the required level of performance.

The gross misconduct stage

This is the ultimate stage of the disciplinary procedure which would either mean that the previous stages of the procedure had been ineffective or that the employee has committed an act of gross misconduct.

If after a full investigation it is decided that this stage of the procedure applies, it can lead to the individual exiting the organization, possibly to a further final warning or perhaps a salary reduction. Again an employee has a full right of appeal and must be made aware of what needs to be done to enable these allegations to be eventually disregarded.

The disciplinary hearing

It will be at this event where each stage of the disciplinary process is discussed and applied.

Before the disciplinary hearing, it must be ensured that a full investigation into the particular case has been undertaken. Factual evidence should be available and the disciplinary hearing should be held as soon as possible after any allegation has been made. Adequate notice of the meeting must be given to the employee, in order to enable him or her to prepare and arrange to be accompanied by either a work colleague or member of their union as required. A suitable venue should be arranged for the meeting, and arrangements must be made for detailed notes to be recorded of the event.

At the start of the hearing, it must be made very clear what the objectives are to be, inevitably to decide whether disciplinary action is appropriate in accordance with agreed procedure. Any allegations should be stated clearly and supported by factual evidence and possibly written statements, if appropriate. Throughout the meeting, the employee must be given a full chance to explain what has happened and give his or her side of the case. Throughout the meeting, regular summarizing should take place so that both local management, Personnel (if involved at this stage) and the employee are very clear about what is being discussed and the progress being made.

The outcome of the disciplinary hearing is to decide what the implications are for the employee concerned. It should be made very clear how long any decision will apply, exactly what levels of performance improvement are required, and what ongoing support and guidance will be available to facilitate the employee's progress. The main factors that determine the eventual penalty for the employee include:

1) The seriousness of the offence.

2) The level of penalty applied in similar disciplinary cases.

3) The employee's previous disciplinary record.

4) To ensure the penalty is fair and reasonable, and seen as such by all parties concerned in this particular case.

As we have mentioned above when discussing the various stages of the disciplinary process, the employee again has a full right of appeal.

After the hearing, it is crucial that a full written record of the event is produced and shared with Personnel and the employee concerned. This written record should include details of the nature of the offence, supporting evidence, what was discussed throughout the disciplinary hearing, the decision that was reached and specific details of the way forward. The written record should also include the agreement for ongoing formal support for the employee, and regular progress reviews.

The employment tribunal

If the disciplinary procedure has led to a member of staff being dismissed, he or she has the right to take an organization to an employment tribunal for unfair dismissal or discrimination.

It is also possible that a member of staff may resign in any case, and then take an organization to an employment tribunal implying constructive dismissal.

Typically, an employee has up to three months to register a claim against an organization.

We have already seen how important it is for an organization to follow any agreed disciplinary procedure, always making accurate documentation at each stage – in the event of an employment tribunal, an organization will be asked to produce all relevant documentation to confirm the course of action it has taken.

As a general rule, an employer must be satisfied that *on the balance of probabilities* an employee was guilty of misconduct warranting dismissal. This means that in a case of unfair dismissal, the onus is on the employer to demonstrate that the employee was dismissed on reasonable grounds. Misconduct is a specific example of such a reason, but in other circumstances the Tribunal needs to be convinced that the employer acted reasonably throughout.

In the case of constructive dismissal, the onus is on the employee to provide proof. Constructive dismissal occurs where an employee has resigned, primarily due to the employer's conduct, giving the employee no other alternative.

The grievance procedure

The objective here is primarily for an organization to maintain positive relationships with its employees.

Grievances can be either informal or formal. Ideally, for interested parties' perspectives, a grievance should be resolved informally – this outcome is usually achieved by the employee discussing his or her concerns with the direct line manager, as appropriate.

Throughout, it is likely that Personnel will be kept fully informed, and sometimes actively involved. In addition, should the formal grievance process be implemented, the employee has the right to be represented and accompanied by a colleague or a representative from a trade union.

As you would expect, accurate and detailed records must be kept throughout the grievance procedure, should any third parties wish to see details (for example, the employee and/or his or her representative).

There are three basic stages to the formal grievance procedure:

Preparation beforehand

- It is essential that the employee has informed the organization, in writing and specifically, what their grievance is.

- It is very likely that Personnel will be kept fully involved, and should be used to seek advice.

- The grievance meeting (or *hearing*) should be arranged as soon as possible after the formal written request has been received from the employee – probably the event should be arranged within 28 days.

- Employees must be given adequate warning of when the meeting is to take place, in order to make adequate arrangements, not only to prepare themselves, but to arrange to be accompanied, should they wish to be so.

- The first grievance meeting is usually held between the employee (and a representative) and the employee's immediate line manager. If the actual grievance is against the line manager concerned, then clearly other suitable arrangements should be made.

- Careful consideration needs to be given to the venue for the meeting and, if appropriate, this venue should be away from the employee's normal place of work.

- As for any meeting, it is essential that full and professional preparation is undertaken, ensuring total familiarity with the facts of the grievance, having a clear plan of action for the meeting and making sure that detailed notes are taken throughout.

The grievance hearing

- At the start of the meeting the agreed purpose of the event should be confirmed.

- Usually the employee then outlines the details of the grievance and all parties concerned should seek clarification as appropriate to ensure that all relevant facts are available and understood. It would be at this stage that any issues should be discussed and clarified.

- Throughout, regular summarizing should take place, because this will ensure that all parties are comfortable with what has been discussed and agreed.

- Possibly, an outcome could be agreed on the day of the meeting, and if so verbal confirmation should be given to the employee.

- It may not be possible to reach a decision on the day of the meeting. In this case, an adjournment may have to be agreed and a date as soon as realistically possible afterwards must be arranged to reconvene.

- When a decision is reached the employee should be advised of the outcome, in writing, within seven days of the meeting itself.

After the grievance meeting

- Ensure that all notes and documentation are checked for accuracy.

- Ensure that written confirmation of the outcome of the meeting is sent to the employer within seven working days of the meeting.

- If appropriate, ensure that copies of all documentation and written confirmation of the outcome of the meeting are sent to the employee's representative.

- Keep copies of all documentation in your own records, in case they are called upon in the future.

What we have outlined above is the informal stage of the grievance procedure, and ideally any issues are solved in that way. We would then proceed to the formal stage, where again it should be hoped that the employee, once advised in writing of the outcome of the meeting, should feel satisfied with the outcome.

If this is not the case, a further meeting/hearing can be requested with a more senior member of the management team. The guiding principles for any such meeting are:

- That the manager concerned be of a higher level than the employee raising the grievance.

- That the manager now involved be of a higher level than the manager involved at the first meeting.

- That the manager involved has had no involvement in either the first meeting or in the case itself.

If again after this second meeting no satisfactory outcome is reached, then a third meeting can be arranged – the guiding principles detailed above still apply – the one difference being, usually, is that any decision reached at this third meeting is final and binding.

INDEX